HUNTING *with the* CAMERA

From *American Water & Game Birds,* courtesy of E. P. Dutton & Co., and Chanticleer Press

A Wilson's Plover settles on its eggs five minutes after the
photographer's companion has left the nesting site.

HUNTING *with the* CAMERA

A Guide to Techniques and Adventure in the Field

ALLAN D. CRUICKSHANK, *Editor*
CHARLES E. MOHR
EDWARD S. ROSS
HERMAN W. KITCHEN
RUTHERFORD PLATT

HARPER & BROTHERS, PUBLISHERS, NEW YORK

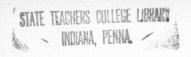
CONTENTS

LIST OF ILLUSTRATIONS

INTRODUCTION

FROM a humble start in 1839 photography has grown steadily to attain a use, respect, and following little dreamed of by its persistent pioneers. It is estimated that there are now more than 25,000,000 camera enthusiasts in North America alone. In just a little over a century photography has become a universal language, and an important medium in communication and clarification. One striking photograph may vividly reveal a scientific fact, demonstrate simplicity of construction, or exemplify graphically artistic principles. Today most of us are decidedly picture conscious. We take it for granted that newspapers, magazines, and books will be richly augmented by outstanding and technically excellent illustrations.

All naturalists admire, and rightly so, those pioneers of wildlife photography who late in the nineteenth and early in the twentieth centuries labored afield with massive cameras, heavy, fragile glass plates, dangerous flash powders, and often large, stuffy portable darkrooms. Equal admiration should be given to the scientists and manufacturers who year after year have produced stronger, simpler, faster, more accurate equipment and materials. Recent improvements in color transparencies and electronic flash are virtually revolutionizing nature camera work and stimulating more and more people to try wildlife photography.

This book is not intended as a manual of photography, but rather as a guide to the techniques of taking still wildlife pictures. It is assumed that the reader has some understanding of the broad fundamentals of photography which have been so clearly and thoroughly stated in numerous photo manuals now on the market.

The title of this book explains its objectives. Experts in six major fields of wildlife photography have written on their specialties. They have presented broad, sound principles which are sure to aid the beginner greatly. At the same time they have sought to impart a feeling of the fun, excitement, and challenge of the field. The circumstances confronting a wildlife photographer are so diverse that any advice must be regarded as a highly elastic suggestion rather than an inflexible rule. The quickest way to become proficient is to photograph and by trial, error, and experience acquire the important know-how. It is hoped the suggestions offered here will send the beginner in the right direction. Once launched on a trail established through generations of careful thought and experimentation by a multitude of wildlife photographers, you can use your own ingenuity to explore the endless possibilities.

Some have stated that the camera is a mechanical instrument and that therefore the photographer deserves little credit for his pictures. They forget that this camera is manipulated by human hands, human eyes, and human brains. The resulting pictures are a reflection of the personality, ingenuity, and ability of the person exposing the film. Photography is essentially creative. It is a form of self-expression. An unusual shot is ordinarily the result of sound judgment and imagination.

While most of this book deals with animal photography, a very important section has to do with plants. Plants are the only things in the world that can actually manufacture food. Directly or indirectly they provide food and shelter for all animals and their interdependence is a basic reality. In fact, all of nature fits into a complex web of life, and one cannot study or photograph one field without including at least part of the others. Regardless of your special interest, it is advisable to read every chapter in this book.

Medical authorities emphasize that one of the surest ways to insure a long happy life is to be absorbed in a hobby, especially one that will keep us outdoors and stimulate our interest in life. Some have compared hobbies to escape valves relieving the nervous tension of the complex problems that now surround us. They consider a hobby as an escape from life. I wonder if this is a sound interpretation. I do not consider my photography as an escape from life, but rather as an entering into life. I am merely taking advantage of the richness and interest afforded to everyone by nature.

Certainly, hunting with the camera meets all the requirements for a satisfying hobby. At the same time it is a constructive form of recreation. Photographs have their place in science since they often show accurately structures and actions which long descriptions, no matter how carefully worded, frequently fail to explain. They have their place in art, not only by portraying artistic principles, but by capturing nature's beauty. They aid in conservation by arousing the interest of more people in nature and strengthening their determination to see that this priceless heritage is protected and wisely used. Wildlife photographs have their place in business when they enhance an advertisement, or add to the value and attractiveness of a magazine or book.

Wildlife photography is a captivating experience. Once the pleasure, excitement, and challenge are experienced you will forever be an enthusiastic devotee.

ALLAN D. CRUICKSHANK

Rockledge, Florida
1957

HUNTING *with the* CAMERA

BIRDS

by Allan D. Cruickshank

BIRD photography is by no means a sport for a select few. Nor is it limited to those who live in the country; I took my first bird photograph at the edge of New York City, the largest city in the world, when I was but a sophomore in high school. The bird photographer knows no closed season, no bag limit, no protected species. He can go out when he wants and as often as he wants with his camera and pass hours trying to trick naturally shy creatures into having their pictures taken. It is an exciting sport. More stalking skill, knowledge of the outdoors, and patience are required by the photographer than by the hunter who can kill his subject at long range.

PRIMARY REQUISITES

The fundamental requirements for success are an understanding of the habits of your subjects, ability to use modern photographic equipment, a creative imagination, extreme patience, and, above all, a determination to succeed. Anyone considering serious bird photography must face the fact that it entails a great deal of thought and work. On rare occasions a good picture may be obtained by sheer luck, but normally hours must be spent stalking subjects, locating nests, erecting blinds, building feeding stations or bird baths, and determining the most satisfactory procedure for tackling a given situation. Frequently hours must be passed in blinds in order to get a single shot of some shy, retiring species. Usually the results are commensurate with the effort put forth. Those who are discouraged easily or who are unwilling to plan meticulously for ever-varying situations should

not attempt bird photography. There will be numerous hard-
ships and many failures. But for the individual who is patient,
who is willing to face disappointments and difficulties, there is
no sport more exciting, more informative, more completely satisfying. Since it not only a year-round sport but one that adds such
interest to life, more and more people with greater leisure time
are taking advantage of this fun and adventure.

ORNITHOLOGICAL KNOWLEDGE

You can begin bird photography with little knowledge of your
subjects, but success will come much faster if you have some ornithological knowledge. The experienced bird watcher will not
waste time looking for the nest of a migrant, or search trees for
the home of a ground-nesting species, or be misled by some bird's
elaborate injury-feigning act. He will know the average degree
of timidity to expect from a given species, its nesting preferences,
its characteristic behavior, and what actions to anticipate.

It does not take long to discover that most birds hide or vanish
as man approaches. This timidity is essential for survival in the
average community. But if you sit still and avoid quick, jerky
motions, birds soon will reappear and proceed with their normal
activities. An alert, patient observer usually has little difficulty
in locating nests. A few elementary facts should be kept in mind.

During the breeding season, if you see a bird repeatedly fly
to a specific bush or clump of grass, it is probable that a nest or
young is the attraction. If you see a bird carrying food or nesting material, you may be certain that by following the bird's
movements you will discover a nest or young. Since field-nesting
birds habitually walk or run long distances after alighting in the
dense grass, nests are located more easily by walking across a field
and watching carefully for the spot from which the bird flushes.
Two people widely separated and dragging a fairly taut line
across the top of the grass in a field often will flush many birds
from their nests. In searching a hedgerow it is always advisable

to walk on the shady side and look toward the light, for any nest will stand out more obviously in silhouette. If a bird such as a killdeer goes through the injury-feigning act, do not follow the bird or even start searching for a nest. The experienced stalker will retreat a long distance, watch the bird through binoculars, and mark the spot where it finally settles to incubate or shelter the young. With a little practice you will quickly learn the tricks and become proficient at nest finding.

After finding a nest leave some definite marker so that you can quickly find it again, but make sure it is not marked so conspicuously or so close to the nest as to attract the attention of predators or even curious people. Often I merely form a small pile of stones for future guidance, or push a stick into the ground ten feet south of the nest.

RESOURCEFULNESS AND HIGH STANDARDS

Photography at nesting sites, though generally the easiest, does not necessarily offer the best possibilities for the most striking pictures. Any place where a bird is likely to return time after time has possibilities. Feeding stations, bird baths, favorite singing perches, flowerbeds frequented by hummingbirds, and shorelines where waders feed or rest—all these offer a challenge for creative work. Never settle in a rut, confining your efforts to one type of situation. Too many photographers restrict their work either to nests or feeding stations. The more types of situations a photographer tackles, the more variety of shots he will obtain and the more interesting will be his collection. Success in obtaining arresting pictures depends more on the resourcefulness and adaptability of the photographer than on his understanding of the technical aspects of photography. Above all, place your standards high. Bear in mind that no matter how frequently a species has been photographed, even by the most expert photographers, you may secure a shot superior to and more interesting than any previous prize.

CAMERA AND ACCESSORIES

Once a subject has been observed repeatedly to visit a nest, feeding station, bird bath, song perch, or any other point, photography becomes chiefly a technical problem. As stated in the introduction, it is not the aim of this book to discuss in detail the technical aspects of photography—lenses, filters, lighting, films, or processing—these subjects have been covered thoroughly in many excellent photo manuals. It is assumed that anyone attempting bird photography will study at least some elementary books on photography and learn the broad fundamentals.

Invariably the beginner will ask which camera to purchase. Ask five experienced bird photographers and you may receive five different answers. It should be stressed that no one camera can cover adequately the whole range of bird photography. Box cameras or other cheap hand cameras equipped only with fixed short-focal-length lenses, and incapable of focusing closer than five feet, are not satisfactory; they will produce too small an image of anything but the largest birds. But the choice of a camera usually is limited by cost. Each individual must decide on the maximum he is justified in spending and buy the best equipment he can get for that price. It is more economical in the long run to start out with the best you can afford.

The chief caution is not to fall for false economy and invest in some cheap make. Insist on a camera manufactured by a company known for its excellent, dependable products. Before investing, study the strength and simplicity of construction of the camera. The life of a naturalist's camera is bound to be a hard, rough one and any suggestion of weakness in construction of an instrument should condemn it. Lightness, compactness, and portability, though unquestionably desirable, must be subordinate to strength and general usefulness.

Different cameras are better suited for different types of work. Each has its advantages and disadvantages. Learn the limitations of your camera and use it only in taking the type of picture for which it is particularly suited. Even the Graflex camera—for years so popular with bird photographers for taking large birds swimming, wading, in flight, or on their nests—has its limitations. It is not satisfactory for work with small birds, since the noise of the mirror snapping out of the way invariably makes the bird jump or turn its head at just the moment the film is being exposed.

For such pictures as flocks of ducks and geese rising from a marsh, herons fishing in a creek, sandpipers and plovers trotting along the shore, vultures sailing overhead, and large birds on their nests, a single-lens reflex type of camera with a sharp telephoto or long-focal-length lens is most satisfactory. The advantage of a reflex camera in such situations is the fact that you can see exactly what you are focused on right up to the instant of exposure and can determine whether the size of the subject is large enough, the focus perfectly sharp, the background satisfactory, and the composition good. Most range finders are unsatisfactory when you are working on fast-moving objects with a telephoto or long-focal-length lens.

Insist on a camera which permits interchangeable lenses, with a wide selection of speeds, and with long bellows extension or its equivalent. Selection, of course, will be governed by the size of negative or transparency desired. Some people prefer 35 mm film; others demand a film as large as 4 x 5. With modern fine-grain black-and-white film or color, the size of the camera is not as important as its ability to produce a large, sharp image of a small object.

When you are working on small birds requiring the use of the camera at very close range, especially when artificial light is preferable or essential, a press or view camera with ground-glass focusing and lens-light synchronization is more satisfactory. Under these conditions the following requirements are essential: (1) ground-glass focusing for absolute sharpness and good composition, (2) interchangeable lenses to meet a variety of situations, (3) long bellows extension or equivalent to permit extreme closeups, (4) a good lens with sharp definition and a wide variety of shutter speeds, (5) ample lens shade, (6) synchronization of lens with type of artificial light to be used, and (7) convenient means of tripping the trigger from a distance.

For those who wish 35 mm negatives or color transparencies, a single-lens reflex camera, or adaptation of a reflex housing on other 35 mm cameras, coupled with a long-focal-length lens, is satisfactory for both large and small birds. When flash is used the camera may be worked from a blind at a distance, and by the use of extensions the flash reflectors set outside the blind, perhaps only two feet from the spot where the subject is expected to alight. The advantage here is that you can check focus and composition right up to the moment of exposure. If an electronic flash is used you can take picture after picture without revealing yourself.

There are great differences of opinion as to the advantages of miniature cameras. I prefer a 3¼ x 4¼ or a 4 x 5 camera, while my wife uses a 35 mm. The miniature camera not only has the advantage of being small, light, and more portable, but film is decidedly cheaper, permitting one to shoot more frequently and more freely. In black-and-white photography the major objection to the 35 mm is the small negative, which requires very careful handling from loading to development and even printing. Each frame is so small that the slightest scratch, fingerprint, or imbedded dust particle will result in a virtually useless enlargement. Moreover, unless special developer is used, the graininess is unattractive. In 35 mm color the grain problem is mostly eliminated, but dust, scratch, and fingerprint problems remain.

I sympathize with the beginner who must select his first camera from the bewildering array of attractive-looking equipment displayed in photography stores today. Advertising material for each brand makes it sound like the buy of the century. Do not rush. Spend at least a month studying the literature and whenever possible the equipment itself. Try to borrow or rent your preferences, use them, and then decide on the one that best meets your special needs. But again, let me repeat, no one camera can do everything, so do not search for the impossible.

Lenses and Care of Equipment

Always bear in mind that the lens is as important, if not more so, than the camera and demand one with sharp definition throughout its field. Remember that the lens is the eye of the camera and actually does the work. If exposure is controlled by the shutter speed of the lens, be sure the lens you buy offers a wide variety of shutter speeds. Do not confuse shutter speed with aperture opening. In spite of intensive advertising by some companies of the speed of a lens because it can be opened to f/1.5, this has little advantage in most still bird photography, for ordinarily you must work at close range on such small creatures and consequently must close the lens down to at least f/5.6 if a satisfactory depth of field is to be obtained. A variety of telephoto and wide-angle lenses, although expensive, add versatility to the outfit and enable you to get shots otherwise impossible.

A good camera and a good lens, regardless of their sturdiness, must be regarded as precision instruments rather than machines and treated carefully at all times. Keep them as clean as possible and check regularly to make sure everything is in perfect working order. Many an unusual shot has been lost because a shutter stuck, a bellows leaked, or flash batteries were too weak to release the shutter.

Tripods

A rigid tripod of medium height having a titling swivel head is essential. For miniature cameras a light one is usually adequate, but do not choose a tripod until you are convinced that you can make exposures of several seconds with positively no vibration. A revolving tilting top is almost indispensable. This must be sturdy and when locked in the desired angle must not budge even a millimeter. Occasionally a good photograph may be obtained with a hand-held camera, but the majority of all good bird photographs are obtained with the camera supported by a good firm tripod. This is particularly true with color film, which is relatively slow and ordinarily requires exposures of less than 1/50 of a second. Use of the tripod assures you that the picture will not be blurred by camera motion.

One advantage of a tripod that should not be overlooked is the fact that it generally prevents you from taking snapshots. The very act of placing the camera on a tripod consumes time and gives you a moment to calm down. As soon as you are composed and begin to study the situation, you establish the foundation for a really worth-while photograph.

As you progress you will find that more than one tripod is virtually a necessity. Obviously a short tripod is most satisfactory for use on ground-nesting birds, while a tall one is needed for photographing nests in tall bushes. For nests above ten feet I often have constructed a very tall tripod made from two-by-fours and used a ladder to set up the camera. In the very highest situation it may be imperative to work from a blind built in a tree or use a tilting top secured to a branch or fastened to a two-by-four nailed between branches or tree trunks. With imagination you can work on almost any nest you find.

When for some good reason the camera is hand held, steadiness is of paramount importance. In fact, it is as important as sharp focusing if a fuzzy image is to be avoided. Try to brace the camera firmly against some part of your body or, better still, against some firm object such as the trunk of a tree, ledge, or sturdy fence railing.

Exposure Meter

A good exposure meter will prove of tremendous help. In color photography it is virtually a necessity, for the latitude of color film is very narrow and a miscalculation of more than one stop in either direction will produce a useless transparency. Study your instrument carefully and understand thoroughly the way it should be used. Be sure the light reading you take before you expose a film is either from the subject itself or a similarly colored and lighted object. Even with a light meter, judgment is required in most situations. The problem of a dark bird on a whitewashed rock, a white bird in dark vegetation, or side lighting, with its resultant hard, contrasty shadows, cannot be solved by the use of the exposure meter alone. Sometimes a compromise may be used. When in doubt favor your subject of primary interest, the bird.

When a rare opportunity that may never be repeated comes, some photographers insure a good picture by bracketing exposures. To bracket you take one picture as the exposure meter indicates, a second shot a half stop over, and a third a half stop under. One of these exposures should be well-night perfect. Unless this technique is limited to unusual opportunities it can become very expensive, especially for those using large films.

Light meters are intricate, delicate precision instruments and should be treated with the utmost care. Never point one directly at the sun, and do not subject it to any unnecessary jarring or damaging shocks.

Binoculars

A pair of prism binoculars is invaluable in searching for nests, watching birds, and checking activities around a situation once the camera has been erected and fixed for remote control. If finances permit, buy a reliable make with central focusing, coated optics, and at least six-power magnification. To insure sufficient light the objectives (front lenses) should have a diameter at least five times the power of the glass. Thus a six-power binocular should read 6 x 30 or more.

Record Book

It is advisable for the photographer to keep accurate records of all exposures: the type of film, aperture, shutter speed, time of day, and lighting conditions. Then by studying the results you will soon evolve a reliable formula for obtaining the best results with your particular outfit.

The photographer has an unusual opportunity to observe un-known or little-known activities of birds at close range. Jot down all interesting observations in a notebook. Do not rely on memory to recall later all that you have seen. These observations written on the spot may add much to ornithological knowledge. Some persons find the keeping of such notebooks as exciting and as valuable as the photography itself.

LARGE BIRDS IN FLIGHT

Occasionally, by using the reflex-type camera with a long-focal-length lens or a 35 mm camera with a long-focal-length lens coupled with a good easily manipulated range finder, pictures of large birds in flight may be obtained while the photographer walks across a field or marsh or rides in a boat, car, or even a plane. Under these conditions, a thorough working knowledge of the camera is essential, for split-second decisions are necessary, permitting no time to deliberate over the correct exposure or the manner of focusing. Every move must be smooth and almost auto-matic and all attention centered on the subject, its actions, and the best composition for catching the feeling of the moment. The experienced bird photographer anticipates the picture possibili-ties and determines in advance the speed and aperture he wishes and the approximate maximum distance at which he will try for a shot. When using black-and-white film for flight shots, always use a filter to avoid a sky that reproduces dead white. With color use a speed fast enough to arrest movement, yet not so fast that the sky will reproduce too dark regardless of a wide aperture.

In all flight shots learn to swing the camera smoothly, following

the movement of the bird, and releasing the shutter while con-
tinuing to follow through. Bear in mind that it is much easier
to stop the motion of a bird in flight if it is coming toward rather
than going parallel to the plane of the film. You soon discover that
it is difficult to focus on a fast-moving bird. Frequently it is
better to decide on the distance you will try for a shot, then set
the camera for that distance, and wait until the bird flies into
focus before releasing the shutter. Superb flight or action shots
are more often the result of good judgment and timing than fast
shutter speed. The photographer anticipates some position,
pause, or suspension of action and trips the trigger at precisely
the right moment.

Even at 1/1000 of a second most birds in flight move ap-
preciably. As a rule only large birds can be stopped sufficiently
for a pleasing picture. A satisfactory image is the chief object.
Some photographers want the bird crystal sharp; others prefer a
slight blur at the wingtips to emphasize movement. This is
strictly a personal preference. Artists differ in opinion as widely
as photographers. Some paint birds in flight as though frozen in
mid-air by an electronic flash; others purposely blur wingtips to
suggest motion. The amount of blurring permissible depends
not only on the attitude of the photographer but to a large
degree on the use to which the negative will be put. A slight
movement that is rather attractive on a contact print may be
decidedly unpleasant when an enlargement is made.

Try to shoot in the direction in which your shadow falls, as this
position automatically prevents sun from shining into the lens.
For flight photography, morning or late afternoon light is preferable to that of midday, for then the underparts of the bird are
more satisfactorily illuminated. The movements of small birds
in flight are so fast that satisfactory shots are generally impossible
without the use of electronic flash. Suggestions on this kind of
flight photography will be found in the section dealing with the
electronic flash (Pages 48-50).

STALKING

Stalking of perched birds is seldom practical. It is generally successful only with a few extraordinarily tame, fearless, or, dare I say, stupid seabirds. But successful or not, stalking gives the photographer some of his keenest enjoyment. Most persons are happier trying to approach a quarry by stealth rather than lying in wait, even though they know in advance that with the former method their chances of success are less.

Stalking in photography differs considerably from the stalking performed by a hunter, as the photographer must get much closer to the quarry. It is wiser for the photographer not to hide, but to approach slowly in full view. Birds, with the most marvelous powers of sight of any creatures in the world, seldom can be closely approached undetected. Even if it were possible to advance close enough unseen, the instant any portion of the photographer or his camera appeared the subject would depart. Remember that nothing alarms a bird more than a sudden jerky motion. It is better to remain in view throughout, slowly approaching, yet acting as though you were not intent on getting near. You should try by your actions to allay any fear. At the slightest suggestion that the subject considers flight, "freeze" or even momentarily retreat a short distance, giving the bird time to regain composure. After you reach the desired spot you must continue to avoid quick jerky motions. It is wise to decide in advance on the approximate distance, aperture, and speed desired so there will be no hesitation or unnecessary movements to alarm the subject at the crucial moment of exposure.

REMOTE CONTROL

In some situations you may find it convenient and satisfactory to place a camera on a tripod and set off the shutter by remote control when the subject is in focus in the correct field. Many excellent shots may be obtained in this manner at a nest, singing perch, feeding station, bird bath, or even along a shoreline. If the shutter is released by means of a long string, be sure to use a strong, dark, nonglossy fishing line with little elasticity and keep it taut so the shutter will trip at precisely the moment desired. Fasten a smooth screw eye near the bottom of one of the tripod legs or drive into the ground directly beneath the camera a peg with a hole near the top. Then pass the release cord through the hole so the pull will be down instead of sideways. This will prevent your overturning the camera in the excitement of releasing the shutter. Better still, use a solenoid or its equivalent with an electric cord and battery for instantaneous release. The battery power required will depend on the type of shutter and the length of the extension cable. When using this technique on very shy birds it is often wise to make a rough dummy camera, such as a tin can nailed on a box, and set it up nearby days in advance of photography. Then move it closer day by day. In this way any bird can be accustomed to the man-made structure and on the day of photography the real camera can be substituted and pictures obtained at close range.

The main objection to remote-control photography is that with most cameras, unless the photographer has unusual mechanical ability, he will have to walk to the camera after each exposure to change the film and recock the shutter. Another difficulty is choosing, from a distance, the exact pose you wish to photograph. You can overcome this latter difficulty, however, by operating the shutter from a blind placed a short distance from the camera. Even the tilt of the bird's head or the highlight in its eye may be the thing that makes the picture exceptional.

PHOTOGRAPHING NESTS AND EGGS

Many people like to have a good collection of photographs showing the nests and eggs of all species they find. Usually the camera tilted at approximately a 45-degree angle will give the least distortion. The best plan is to use a tripod, carefully focus on the front edge of the nest with the lens wide open, and then close down far enough to bring the back of the nest and eggs into sharp focus. Frequently the eggs will have to be grouped at the very back of the nest if they are to appear in the picture. For the thoughtful photographer, nest photography has numerous ramifications. Some pictures may be taken from above to show the contents and inside structure; some on a level to reveal depth, shape, and outside construction; and some from the most pleasing angle to portray beauty. In some instances careful composition and a small lens aperture may be used to tie the nest of the species to its habitat preference.

BLINDS

Importance of the Blind

Occasionally, in unusual nesting colonies such as the gannet cliffs of Bonaventure Island off the Gaspé Peninsula in Canada, or at places like the Anhinga Trail in the Everglades National Park where birds are surprisingly confiding, you may take pictures to your heart's content without thought of concealment. But since most birds are shy and difficult to approach, you must ordinarily work in a blind or hide if you wish to photograph at close range. A good blind is of utmost importance. Some persons argue that with modern photographic techniques which enable you to trip the trigger by remote control, a blind is unnecessary. Nevertheless, in most situations I still prefer to use a blind, as it is the only way to be really close to my subjects with assurance that they will go about their usual activities in a normal manner. Not only do I want to see everything that is going on to satisfy my ornithological interest, but I want to select carefully the pose to photograph. As that splendid bird artist, Francis Lee Jaques once remarked, "A bird is not graceful in all of its poses." I always try to obtain not only good composition but a graceful pose typifying some characteristic posture. Furthermore, to me the intimate contact a blind permits is as thrilling as the photography itself. It is an unforgettable experience when some shy bird comes to its nest or a pond's edge at only arm's length from the blind, quite oblivious to the presence of the photographer. Under these conditions you often can observe every detail of courtship, ceremonial dances, incubation rhythms, territorial fights, feeding of the mate or young, and other behavior that really makes bird watching so intriguing. Years have passed since my first use of a blind and I have seen hundreds of birds return to their nests; yet the experience remains forever fresh and thrilling.

Types of Blinds

Anything that conceals the photographer and does not frighten the subject may be used as a blind. In emergencies I have hidden in cars, pup tents, large boxes, hollow trees, canoes, caves, or shallow excavations covered with branches. Once, when barn owls nested in an old deserted attic, I fixed a hiding place in a large pile of rubbish. Generally, however, it is much more convenient to carry an ever-ready, light, easily erected portable tent or blind roughly three feet square and four to six feet tall. Years ago photographers went to great trouble in creating blinds resembling natural objects. One of the most distinguished of these was the famous English photographer, Richard Kearton, who successfully used a dummy ox as a blind. In my beginning years I used one blind that resembled an old tree trunk and another that looked like a grass mound. Experience has proved that such elaborate imitations are not only heavy and awkward to handle but totally unnecessary. Most birds quickly accept any object as long as it is sturdy enough not to shake in the wind, opaque enough to conceal the photographer, and tight enough so as not to flap and frighten the subject.

In the last decade I have seen scores of satisfactory blinds used by different photographers. Each photographer has his favorite; the beginner will have to experiment until he decides which type of blind is most convenient for his personal use.

Years ago an umbrella blind was conceived, and numerous writers have mentioned it since. This consists of an umbrella with green cloth sides. It is suspended by an adjustable jointed brass rod pointed at the base so it can be pushed into the ground easily. I never recommend this type of blind, as it is virtually impossible to use in a windy situation. In fact, with the slightest breeze the sides shake and flap, thereby frightening the subject. Moreover, the supporting pole placed in the middle of the blind is a constant obstacle and annoyance.

Frequently in remote-control photography I use an automobile as a blind. Birds seem to assume that people in cars mean no harm, and will go about their normal activities as long as the photographer sits still. In emergencies in remote places I have used an easily constructed blind composed solely of three poles gathered in the field and tied together at the top to form a tripod. Over this a piece of brown or green burlap is draped to form a

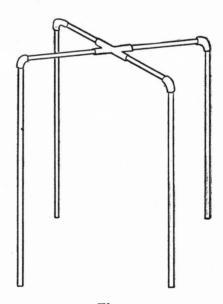

Fig. 1

tepee and pinned tightly. Another cheap, easy to construct, and more satisfactory framework consists of four uprights six feet tall driven into the ground at each corner of a three-foot square and linked together at the top with galvanized wire. The base of the poles should be pointed so they may be driven into the ground with greater ease.

A ready-made, quick-assembling, self-supporting framework is always preferable and often will help the photographer obtain pictures he might otherwise miss. Figure 1 illustrates a simple, easily constructed framework. The metal one-inch piping is cut, threaded, and screwed together by elbows and central cross. The uprights are six feet long. The framework is three feet square at both top and base. All threaded parts should be kept well greased to prevent complications from rusting.

At present my favorite blind is a duraluminum framework designed and given me by the excellent motion-picture photographer Bayard Read. It consists of only four light pieces which fit together quickly. It is shown in Figure 2.

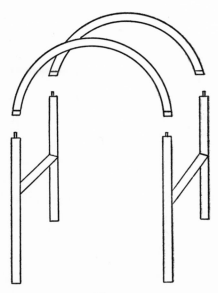

Fig. 2

The light weight is of great convenience when you must carry the blind for a distance. The noncorrosive metal is desirable as it will withstand constant rough treatment. The quick assemblage is most important, as the birds are disturbed as little as possible. A disadvantage is the fact that the rig cannot be broken down into a small bundle for transportation in limited space, but with some mechanical tinkering you can quickly rearrange the construction to remedy this problem.

Blind Cover

The cover of any blind must be opaque enough so the photographer is invisible even when he is directly between the subject and the sun. If movements within are noticeable to a shy bird, it will refuse to come near. Years ago I made my blind cover with artificial grass bought from funeral parlors or cemeteries, but this material is not only extremely heavy and bulky but unnecessary. Burlap sewed in double thickness or bark cloth (used for slip covers) is more satisfactory. Bark cloth not only has the advantage of less bulk but it is much lighter since only one thickness is necessary. Green, brown, or gray colors make the blind less conspicuous on the landscape and may be helpful in keeping curious persons from coming to examine the setup when you least want any visitors.

The most easily constructed cover consists of two 17-foot lengths of yard-wide material sewed together to form a cross, as shown in Figure 3.

Sew three sides firmly together to within a foot of the bottom. Use a brass zipper or safety pins to close the fourth corner or entrance. Make sure the cover fits snugly, as the flapping of cloth frightens most wild creatures.

Lens Opening and Observation Slits

For the lens opening a 42-inch slit on one side closed with a double brass zipper, one slide moving up from below, the other

1. Laughing Gulls gliding over a Texas sea wall hang suspended in updraft.

2. Western Gull at a California beach cannot decide whether to allow closer approach by the photographer.

3. Wood Ibis returning from feeding grounds to nesting colony stream over the photographer's blind in Florida.

4. Synchronized lens-flash is set off by remote-control as Screech Owl eyes the equipment set up outside its nesting cavity.

5. A suspicious Snowy Egret runs past the photographic blind.

6. A White-throated Sparrow is coaxed before the camera by grain
sprinkled in crevice of a fallen tree trunk.

7. The photographer hid in a blind for hours to obtain this picture of an
American Egret feeding its young.

sliding down from above, allows the photographer to place his camera at any height desired within those 42 inches. Then he can zip the opening until it closes snugly around the lens.

I have found observation slits on each side of the blind most convenient. These, of course, must be very narrow. The following type is both strong and effective. Cut a slit four inches long at the desired place. Cover this opening with a double thickness of plastic or fiberglass screening about six inches long and two inches wide. Carefully turn in the edges of the slit fabric so no raw edges remain and the opening is no more than a quarter-inch wide.

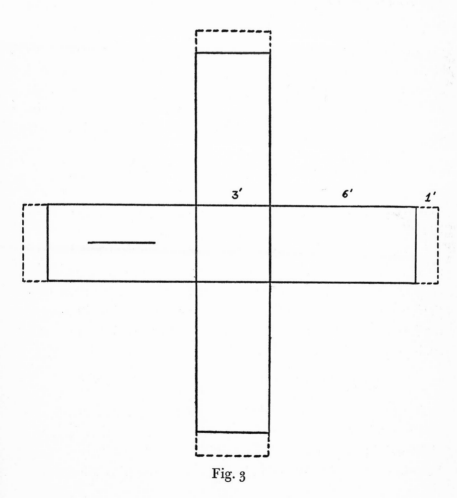

Fig. 3

Sew together the fabric and the screening around the opening and sew again around the outside edge of the screening. If desired, reinforce this with rug-weight iron-on Bondex tape, available at most ten-cent stores and notion counters. These narrow slits enable the photographer to see clearly everything going on outside, yet keep him securely hidden from the keenest and most suspicious subject. Caution should be taken to prevent too much light from entering the blind. The darker it is within, the less noticeable will be the movements of the photographer.

Anchoring the Blind

The extra flaps at the bottom of each side of the cover are very useful. With these flaps spread on the ground, weights such as stones, logs, or even sand may be piled on to hold the blind rigid against the onslaughts of wind. In very windy situations, especially on hard ground where the framework legs cannot be pushed into the earth, heavy weights are imperative. When the wind is exceptionally strong, guy ropes securely anchored by rocks or with tent pegs are advisable. Before you hide in a blind be sure it will not move if the wind increases. It is disconcerting to say the least, after waiting hours for some rare shot, to have the blind topple over at the crucial moment.

In open, windy situations a blind only four feet tall is often preferable, but whenever possible avoid crowding yourself, camera, tripod, and stool into a smaller space or you may experience some agonizing hours. You can crouch, bend or kneel for fifteen minutes or half an hour, but after that length of time such positions become unbearable.

Seat for the Blind

A strong folding stool that will take rough treatment and not creak is of utmost importance. Be sure, too, that it is the right height so you may sit motionless for long periods without becoming cramped. We can all endure intense discomfort when a difficult or unexpected situation demands it, but every effort should be made to eliminate unnecessary fatigue in order that attention can be centered on acquiring excellent pictures. Some birds are slow and deliberate and the photographer must "freeze" for long periods. Unless he is physically comfortable he is likely to develop cramps or find that his legs go to sleep and prickle intolerably with pins and needles. Frequently the difference between success and failure depends on the ability of the photographer to sit motionless for a long period of time, yet remain at peak alertness.

Setting Up the Blind in Advance

Often I find it wise to erect blinds at three or four different nests in one day and give the birds time to become accustomed to the structures before I attempt photography. Some species will accept a blind as soon as it is erected and the photographer has disappeared. With very shy species it may be necessary to place the blind 100 feet away and then gradually move it closer. If the photographer is patient and takes days to accomplish the act, the shyest birds will eventually accept a blind placed only a few yards away.

A blind tends to arouse the curiosity of people as well as horses and cattle. Be sure not to leave an expensive blind in a place where it may be torn apart or stolen. In pastures it is wise to drive stakes around an area including the blind and nest and enclose the area with strong wire. Unless this precaution is taken, cows or horses will investigate and trample the nest or knock over the blind.

Blind de Luxe

At feeding stations, bird baths, or shorelines where photography is carried on for weeks or even years, blinds de luxe may add great comfort and convenience. Here a permanent structure covered with tar paper or even shingling will keep the inside dry. A friend of mine near New York City used a well-constructed waterproof shed four feet square and six feet tall with a cement floor and added a heating device for cold days. The possibilities for comfort and convenience are endless.

Procedure at a Nest

Once the blind is in place and the camera equipment assembled on the tripod, tie back or weigh down any branches between the lens and the nest. If the nest is on a slender branch which waves in the wind, you should steady the branch by anchoring it with ropes tied to pegs in the ground. Only when no other solution is possible should a piece of vegetation be cut away. When you complete your picture taking it is your responsibility to leave the nest surroundings in as near their original undisturbed condition as possible. Always consider that the safety of the bird and the nest contents are of paramount importance.

Check carefully to make sure that no branch or blade of grass can swing into the picture once you are in the blind, and that none of the grasses or leaves around the nest present distracting highlights. Then focus carefully, compose, check the light reading with your meter, and be sure all films and accessories you will need are within easy reach in the blind. Remember that right-handed people find it most convenient to sit in the left rear corner of the blind. Remember, too, that it is much easier to focus on the front edge of the nest, feed log, or bath with the lens wide open and then close down to the desired aperture. Before you settle down in the blind be sure everything is the way you want it; later correction may ruin your chances of success.

Cooperative Companion Helpful

The length of time the photographer may have to wait will vary according to the species. Some gulls and terns alight on the nest and even on the blind five minutes after the photographer has settled within, even though no walk-away companion is present to convince them that danger has gone. But with very shy species it is helpful to have a companion who will walk away with sufficient noise so the creature is aware of his departure. Most birds apparently fail to distinguish between two people approaching and one leaving. They seem to register only that danger is approaching and danger is leaving.

No matter how urgent the situation, the photographer never should walk suddenly out of the blind, thus startling his subject. Such a sudden appearance will often so frighten the bird that it will refuse to return to the nest until the blind has been removed. Arrange some system of signals if you have a companion. If a branch has snapped up or fallen between the camera and the subject and must be weighed down out of the field, it is best that the companion approach, act as a distraction, and if possible correct the situation and then walk away. A signal my wife and I use is the corner of a white handkerchief pushed through a hole at the top rear of the blind. When displayed this means a call for help.

It is unwise to decide in advance on a definite time when the companion should return to relieve you or take his turn in the blind. Invariably he will come just at the moment you are about to take some unusual shot. Decide on an approximate time, but have it understood that the companion is not to approach unless the signal is displayed. While the photographer is spending long hours in the blind, the companion can follow his own inclinations: perhaps photograph insects, flowers, scenes, large birds in flight, or search for the nests of species still needed in the photographic collection.

At the end of any job when I am working alone or with birds not particularly timid, I persuade them to depart without fear by making a noise or shaking the blind before I reveal myself. This prevents startled leaps from the nest that could endanger eggs or young.

Keeping Calm

I doubt if anyone can forget his first experience in a blind. Every nerve tingles as the bird approaches. The photographer finds himself holding his breath and tensely handling his release cable. There is to me no experience more exciting. My only warning is, do not be trigger-happy. Do not snap pictures in rapid succession at the first opportunity. It is better to wait, observe the actions of the bird for a while, allow the subject to gain confidence, and decide which pose you want most before exposing any film. Often a bird has a set trail it uses in approaching its nest. Certain perches it habitually uses may well offer more striking pictures than those on the nest.

Other Kinds of Blind Work

Photography from a blind at very close range is not confined to nests. In other situations more skill and imagination may be required, but the results are worth the additional thought and effort. A blind placed at a feeding station or bird bath will offer unusual opportunities. A blind set at a carefully chosen point on the edge of a mud flat or marsh frequented by birds is sure to give the cameraman a wide choice of photographic possibilities. And what great opportunities there are in the dancing grounds of prairie chickens, the drumming log of a ruffed grouse, or the favorite singing perch of a mockingbird! In most situations, except for a specific early morning or later afternoon job, the camera opening of the blind should face north in order to give the maximum hours of photography with the sun at your back. Direct lighting is most essential in color photography. Side lighting and back lighting, while often producing exceptional shots, require remarkable judgment and frequently a large measure of good fortune.

Blinds over Water or in Tall Trees

Occasionally, as at a grebe's nest, it may be necessary for the photographer to work from a blind placed in a boat in deep water. Whenever possible try to wedge the boat firmly into weeds. If this is impossible or unsatisfactory, drive long poles into the mud around the boat to steady it. In most shallow water or marsh situations I find it more satisfactory to drive stakes into the mud, build a sturdy platform, and place the blind on that.

In tall trees you can build a blind at any height. The photographer must study each situation and decide on the best spot and the best way to erect his hideaway.

When construction is necessary in a marsh or tall trees and a shy species is involved, it is prudent to build the floor first and let the birds become accustomed to that. Then bit by bit add the supports, the sides, and the roof. Often I have taken as long as a week to build a single blind. The effort and patience are absolutely necessary to insure success with an extremely nervous subject.

A few species of birds, such as eagles, ospreys, peregrine falcons, and great horned owls, generally use the same nest year after year; the blinds beside such nests may be left in place therefore and used repeatedly.

The possibilities are endless and make this kind of photography forever stimulating. The challenge to photograph successfully what at first seems impossible is a stimulus to imaginative action.

BIRD FEEDING STATIONS

Feeding stations offer excellent year-round locations for bird photography. Good shots at the conventional tray or bird feeder are interesting and always in demand. But a few such poses are generally sufficient and continued shots tend to become

stereotyped and monotonous. Moreover, there are many disadvantages at ordinary feeding stations for the photographer
who demands artistic pictures. Large masses of food are un-
sightly. Many feeding trays are so deep as to hide the bird's
legs and feet. Few feeding trays are objects of beauty, yet they
fill a certain and sometimes a large part of bird photographs
taken at them.

Here imagination and artistic ability can be put to use. Food
placed on some natural-looking rustic log attracts birds just
as quickly as does food on a flat, angular board. You will find
it most satisfactory to select a log that is fairly narrow and short
so that no matter where the bird alights it is automatically in
the field of the camera and in focus. A log set approximately
three to four feet above the ground is at a convenient height
for camera manipulation. Establish feeding stations well in
advance, keep them constantly supplied with food, and give
the birds sufficient time to become accustomed to the cafeteria
before starting photography. I have used a blind at some feeding stations, sat exposed in the garden while working at others,
and even relaxed in the comfort of the house while working
at still others in winter.

The observant photographer soon will notice that a bird
will frequently use specific branches as it approaches the feeding station. By training the camera on one of these perches,
an endless variety of photographs may be obtained. Before se-
lecting a perch, keep in mind that the effectiveness of most
pictures lies in their simplicity.

"What food shall I use?" is a universal question. This will
depend largely on your own location and the species of birds
coming to the feeder. Most advertised mixtures of bird food
are satisfactory. I find fine cracked corn or chick feed is almost
universally liked. Black-capped chickadees generally prefer sunflower seeds, blue jays peanuts, downy woodpeckers beef suet,
and practically all birds that respond to feeding shelves eat
broken nut meats greedily. Mutton suet is shunned by most

species. As a rule, the more variety of food you offer, the greater variety of birds you will attract.

When attracting birds to a given area, be liberal and even extravagant with bird food. But when the birds have become accustomed to food offered in a particular place and it is time to begin photography, use as little food as possible, all of it concentrated in one spot where you wish the bird to perch. If many feeding stations are maintained in one area, during the period of photography cover all except the spot at which you are working, thus forcing all birds in the neighborhood to concentrate at the desired feeder.

The feeding station idea has endless ramifications. Beef suet may be tucked away in the crevices of some picturesque tree trunk; carcasses collected along the highways may be placed beneath an attractive perch in an area frequented by vultures, condors, or eagles. Grain may be tossed near the shore of some attractive lagoon regularly visited by ducks and geese. Dead fish may be anchored in a shallow pool to attract a variety of sandpipers and plovers.

BIRD BATHS

The drinking fountain or bird bath is another place where photography may be carried on throughout the year. As with feeding shelves, a few good shots of birds at conventional bird baths are interesting and always in demand. But you soon exhaust the possibilities of the ordinary cement bath or tin tray seen in most gardens. Why not build your own bird bath so that it looks like a small natural pool with charming native plants growing about it? It will be helpful if three sides of this pool are too high and straight for most birds to use, while the fourth side slopes gradually and is arranged to attract birds to that particular area. The constuction of your bird bath will require careful thought and planning. You will find it most satisfactory to have the fourth side small enough so that no matter where the bird alights there are photographic possibilities. Unless artificial light is to be used exclusively, the bath must be placed in a sunny spot, the sloping side lying on the north to provide the greatest number of hours with direct sunlight. Species present in an area for long periods soon learn where the bath is located; but to attract more of the migrants that pause for brief periods during their journeys north or south, have some dripping water, which immediately informs a newcomer of the presence of drinking water and a refreshing bath. Such a bath is not only doubly attractive to wild creatures, but if carefully arranged it adds greatly to the charm and beauty of the garden.

USE OF FLASH

In days gone by flash was avoided by bird photographers, as the use of flash powder was too noisy, produced too much smoke, and in wilderness areas was a potentially dangerous fire hazard. But with the invention of modern flash devices those objections vanished. Many people are astonished when they discover that modern brilliant, noiseless artificial lights have practically no disturbing effect on most birds. The birds seem to accept this light as a natural phenomenon. Flash photography permits work not only on nocturnal subjects but in situations where the sunlight is so weak that obtaining good pictures under natural conditions is virtually impossible. Frequently the use of flash is helpful to reinforce daylight and light up heavy shadows. Moreover, in most cases strong sunlight on eggs or young birds for extended periods is harmful (*two minutes of full sunlight is enough to kill newly hatched passerine birds*), and the use of flash at a time of day when the nest is in dull light is not only safer but usually results in photographs of better quality. Another advantage that must not be overlooked is the fact that flash standardizes the light factor and enables you to develop through trial and error an almost foolproof standard exposure scale to be used with any given equipment.

With large birds the light must be distributed over such

extensive areas that the advantage of practical artificially produced light is greatly reduced. Moreover, larger birds not only
tend to frequent more open situations but they are normally
slower and more deliberate than small species, thus permitting
much slower exposures. With small birds the light output from
a small artificial source can be concentrated to produce illumination many times greater than the sun. This permits the use
of fast shutter speeds and small apertures seldom or never possible otherwise. The faster the shutter speed, the more motion it
will arrest. Likewise, the smaller the aperture, the greater the
depth of field and over-all sharpness of the image. These two
advantages are especially important when you are working
very close, as is necessary if images of satisfactory size are to
be obtained of small birds. Using flash with fast speeds and a
small aperture in dark places helps avoid double images.

The flash equipment you should obtain again will depend
on the type of camera you use, the speeds at which you plan
to work, and the amount of money you feel you can spend.
There are many good outfits on the market. Make sure the one
selected is made by a company of good repute, is synchronized
with your shutter, and that there is some means of remote control. In all types of photography better illumination and modeling result when the light comes from two or more directions;
therefore, provision should be made for the use of a second
or even third flash head.

But even flash bulbs have limitations. Remember that at
speeds of 1/100 or 1/200 of a second small birds must be practically motionless if they are to be arrested on film. When you
are familiar with certain species of birds you will be able to
anticipate the moment when convenient pauses will occur. With
or without flash I often use the simple trick of giving a slight
hiss or snap of the fingers just before releasing the shutter.
This faint sound tends to make the birds pause or "freeze"
while the film is being exposed.

In flash work a blind concealing the camera creates decided

handicaps. It is better when using a blind to place it back from the camera and use remote control to set off the flash. With sufficiently remote operation a blind is often unnecessary. In such situations make certain in advance that the subject can be seen clearly from the place where you plan to operate the release. Even if it is not necessary, I prefer to use a blind in most cases. The blind enables the photographer to station himself close enough to see clearly every motion of the bird and choose carefully the pose he likes best. The experienced photographer is not trigger-happy. He waits for the bird to assume a desirable pose. Experience has taught him that most pictures of birds looking into or away from the camera are useless. A profile or side view is generally preferable, although, as in all rules, there are exceptions. With flash it is wise for the beginner to keep careful records of his technique. These initial trials will establish a sound formula for all later calculations.

Electronic Flash

There are three major types of artificial light. The photoflood and photoflash techniques, although excellent in their respective fields, are relatively slow and are governed by the mechanical operation of the shutter. In recent years the perfection of the electronic flash tube permits the stopping of the smallest bird in rapid motion. Here the exposure is not limited by the mechanical operation of the shutter, but is determined solely by the duration of the flash, often 1/10 the time of maximum shutter speed. An outfit that gives a flash of 1/5000 of a second or faster is preferable. Special sets produce a flash hundreds of times brighter than sunlight; some have a duration of but one microsecond (1/1,000,000 of a second). These fast speeds allow a clear, sharp image regardless of the activity of the subject. At present the initial cost of a satisfactory fast electronic flash outfit is one major disadvantage to the average amateur bird photographer. If many flash pictures are taken, however, the cost per shot is much less. Another disadvantage of electronic flash is that there are more possibilities of things going wrong. Unless you are exceptionally well informed in the fields of mechanics and electronics, you frequently may find yourself in difficulties.

With ordinary flash it is a problem to stop quick action, but with electronic flash you can stop the action even of small birds in flight, as they land, or as they take off. The major problem here is to trip the trigger at the precise moment when the bird is in focus in the narrow field of the camera. With great concentration and planning this can be done manually in many cases, but one will find that all too frequently he trips the trigger just before the bird has entered the picture or after it has landed or passed out of the narrow field. This problem can be solved by a photoelectric circuit that trips the trigger at precisely the moment when the bird flies through a light beam. But bear in mind that the interruption of such a beam can take place at any point outside the camera field or area in focus. For foolproof perfection some photographers use a second light beam which crosses the first at the exact point they wish to photograph. Thus only simultaneous interruption of both beams will release the trigger, and barring some accidental one-in-a-million occurrence the only place this can happen is where the beams cross.

With the electronic flash many spectacular photographs can be obtained and many amazing movements of a bird revealed. The door to a new picture world has been opened. But a word of caution is in order. Unless he is working on some specialized technical study, the photographer should refrain from trying to get nothing but unusual poses which the human eye never perceives. A few such pictures in a collection are striking, but a display of one such picture after another borders on a freak show. At present the novelty of the unusual is arresting (and details of wing positions are useful in studying flight), but in the long run a collection of pictures predominantly of birds in their characteristic poses and activities as the human eye sees them is much more pleasing to the eye and much more useful.

Flash Background Problems

In all flash photography, particularly in color, the background is a problem. The light may illuminate the chief subject perfectly, yet most of the background may remain coal black. Some such pictures are strikingly beautiful, but all too frequently dark sections of the subject disappear into the black background. The best way to solve this problem is to make sure some vegetation is directly behind the bird and close enough to be illuminated by the flash. You can erect a blue or green piece of cardboard, blotter, or cloth directly behind the place where the subject will be. This will give the general effect of a sky or foliage background which in many instances is pleasing. You must experiment and select a shade that will look as natural as possible in reproduction. Yet, with the utmost care, there is an artificial flavor to such a background. All air seems to be squeezed from behind the bird. I recommend the use of such unnatural backgrounds be kept to a minimum in any collection. Certainly backgrounds of red, yellow, orange, and other unlikely colors which I have seen used by some photographers should be shunned. Whenever possible it is better to select the photographic situation so the surrounding vegetation gives a natural background.

Choose one that is either contrasting enough, complementary enough, or entirely out of focus so that the subject will stand out. In all phases of color work do not permit a desire for maximum amount and variety of color to overpower sound judgment. As in black-and-white photography, the effectiveness of a picture often is the result of its simplicity.

This brings up the common question as to whether backgrounds should be in or out of focus. There are vociferous proponents of each school of thought. Backgrounds can be in or out of focus—the best results often depending on the effect desired or the importance of the background. Each has its merits, as exemplified by the fact that artists who can easily paint what they wish produce some backgrounds showing every detail while others paint merely a hazy suggestive setting. In any case there is no excuse for the principal subject and its immediate surroundings not being absolutely sharp. As a rule it is decidedly better to have the subject fill the major portion of a picture, thus automatically masking excessive background details.

ETHICS IN BIRD PHOTOGRAPHY

Over the years bird photographers, through self-criticism, discussions with colleagues, and printed articles, have built up a now well-established code of ethics which most follow conscientiously.

The first rule of this code is that every precaution be taken to make sure that no subject is endangered by the photographer. No photograph, no matter how beautiful or how unique or rare, is worth sacrificing the life of a bird or the success of a nest. When working on colonial (gregarious nesting) species or any nest directly exposed to the sun, it is imperative to set up the blind early in the morning and hide therein before the heat of the day becomes powerful enough to cook the exposed eggs or delicate young. If you must leave before the nests are in shade, it is your duty to dismantle the blind and camera equipment rapidly and depart from the nesting area in the greatest haste. In situations where branches or clumps of grass must temporarily be tied back or weighed down, care must be taken to restore the natural look of the area when photography is finished. No nest should be removed from its original perch or permanently exposed. The beginner must be particularly careful. With experience you will learn what can be done without endangering the subjects.

I usually urge beginners to work first at bird baths and feeding stations. By doing so they become accustomed to their cameras, and to the techniques necessary in the specialized field of bird photography, under conditions where they can do no harm. Photography at nests, either of individual birds or in the dense concentrations of bird colonies, ordinarily should be left to the experienced photographer who knows his business so well that the birds are little disturbed by his activity.

Even at feeding stations there are ethics to keep in mind. Feeding stations tend to influence some birds to stay far north of their normal wintering grounds. Therefore, once a station has been established and birds induced to remain in an area for the winter, the station must be maintained well into spring when the natural food of the species fed is once more abundant. Even a few days of neglect in frigid spells can be disastrous. Be sure to have the stations well supplied in time of deep snow or ice storms, as many of the wintering guests may be entirely dependent on your food for survival.

Since it is not impossible to photograph any bird or virtually any mammal in the wild, those who specialize in bird and mammal photography generally agree that the subject must be in a wild state, free to move as it wishes. It is true that most feeding stations and baths are man-made setups, but they are out of doors and the bird or mammal is free to come and go as it likes— or stay away altogether. It seems almost superfluous to say that mounted birds should not be photographed and offered as examples of wildlife photography. Yet in years gone by one or two unscrupulous photographers have tried this deceit. Naturalists frown on pictures of mounted birds used as wildlife illustrations, no matter how expert the taxidermist, no matter how ideal the setting in which the specimen is placed.

It is understandable that occasionally someone's pet or a slightly injured creature may be too inviting to resist. I have taken such pictures as a slightly injured snowy owl on Long Island and an exhausted pomarine jaeger found resting on a Florida beach. Negative jacket and prints from such negatives should be labeled so as to indicate captured status. Occasionally a magazine or newspaper will omit this statement in the caption or credit line, but the photographer has the satisfaction of knowing he has not been guilty of faking since the print reproduced had on its label all pertinent information about the conditions under which the photograph was made. In any case, you should habitually avoid photographing captive birds. If you concentrated on exhausted, tame, or confined subjects, you might as well do all of your photography in a zoological park or indoor studio. Pictures of controlled birds or mammals invariably show an artificial touch. Moreover, the thrill of bird photography diminishes in direct proportion to the tameness of the subject. It is the satisfaction of obtaining pictures of alert wild creatures, the challenge of matching your wits with an elusive, unapproachable subject, that gives wild-animal photography a spice unparalleled by any other type of camera work.

Scientific laboratories working on special research problems of bird behavior, studies of flight, and underwater actions of diving birds often use controlled subjects. They produce beautiful illustrations of high scientific merit, but they are frank about the methods used and make no attempt to portray the results as examples of wildlife photography. Some photographers are employed specifically to photograph pets or subjects in zoological parks. Others enjoy zoo photography as a hobby. No criticism is leveled at such work. It is aimed only at those who try to deceive the public and present their results as examples of pictures taken in the wild.

PHOTOGRAPHING YOUNG BIRDS

The only exception to the preceding part of the wildlife code seems to be the photography of young birds. For decades it has been an accepted practice to line up young birds on a branch or other perch to show the whole brood. Such shots are obviously posed, as young birds out of the nest rarely if ever would bunch so closely. There is no attempt to disguise the fact that the photographer placed his subjects in some artistic setting. But let no one assume that obtaining such pictures is easy. The primary response of young birds is to jump off the perch. Get one bird to perch satisfactorily, and as soon as the second bird is raised to position number one jumps off. Most photographers soon give up in despair. The photographer who can persuade seven young chickadees to line up side by side and then make all seven turn sideways with an alert expression at the same moment deserves great credit for his patience. Failure to obtain a picture of some shy adult bird after a whole day of waiting in a blind is not a fraction as exasperating as even an hour's struggle with two or three small fluffy young obstinately refusing to remain on the photography perch. With certain warblers and sparrows the young may eventually accept the perch upon which they have been repeatedly placed, settle down there, and give the hunger call. Then from a blind or by remote control the photographer can make shots of the parent birds coming to feed the begging young. Some of my most satisfactory shots have been obtained in this way.

ENTERING PRIVATELY OWNED LAND

Most photographers find occasions when they wish to work on privately owned lands. In such situations always get permission to enter. Most landowners are generous and hospitable once the project is explained to them. Rightfully, many are annoyed when they see a stranger tramping across their land, and furious when they see someone erecting a queer-looking tent on their property. Likewise, never enter a sanctuary or wildlife preserve until you have obtained permission from the authorities in charge. These acts of courtesy may be time-consuming but they will prevent some unhappy experiences, will allow you to work at ease in any chosen situation, and, as with all acts of politeness, will pay dividends in the end.

MAMMALS

by Allan D. Cruickshank

THE fundamental approaches to mammal photography are similar to those used in obtaining pictures of birds. To acquire a well-rounded collection of wild-mammal pictures, however, is more of a challenge, since mammals have greater mental powers than birds, and most are either nocturnal, secretive, or highly suspicious of man. In most areas this wariness is necessary for their very survival. The amount of camera work possible with such subjects in urban and suburban areas is limited. Some striking pictures may be obtained in these locations, but to do serious work on a great variety of species you must go into wilder places.

PRIMARY REQUISITES

You may be justly proud of a good collection of mammal photographs. As in bird photography, far more knowledge of the outdoors, stalking skill, patience, perseverance, and capacity for exacting work are required by the photographer than by the hunter who can bring down his game from a long distance. Like most fields of nature photography, it is a year-round sport. There are no closed seasons, no bag limits, and no protected species.

The more types of situations you tackle, the more interesting will be your collection and the greater satisfaction it will provide. Do not settle in a narrow rut. Try all types of photography. Work on all kinds of mammals. You must understand basic photography and be able to use your camera correctly, but arresting results will depend more on your imagination, adaptability, and determination than on technical photographic knowledge. Hours must be spent stalking wary subjects; locating nests, dens, burrows; establishing feeding stations and drinking pools; erecting blinds; and deciding on the best way to tackle ever varying situations. There will be many disappointments and numerous failures, but these merely fill the true wildlife photographer with greater determination to obtain some seemingly impossible shot. Be proud of your prize pictures, yet never be completely satisfied. Keep alive the feeling that given another opportunity you can improve on each picture you have taken.

KNOWLEDGE OF MAMMALOGY

A person with little knowledge of mammalogy can get pictures of gray and fox squirrels in city parks, chipmunks and woodchucks in state parks, and a few large game mammals in national parks and wildlife refuges. Some pictures, too, may be snapped in the wilds by a fortunate sequence of events. But to achieve an outstanding collection demands serious study of your subjects and knowledge of where to find and what to expect from each species. If you want to photograph a certain mammal, determine its range, areas of highest population density, habitat requirements, and food preferences. Is it chiefly nocturnal or diurnal? At what season will its fur appear best and its antlers large and impressive? What is the temperament of the average individual, and what behavior should you anticipate?

Beginners must be cautioned immediately to regard large mammals with respect. Some species are temperamental and their actions unpredictable. There are bad-tempered individuals even in normally trustworthy species. Regardless of species, never get between a bear and her cub. A photographer friend of mine who did so was chased up a tree, and the angry mother ripped off his big toe. Bull moose must be approached with caution. Some will eye a human with only slight interest. Others, especially at the height of the rutting season in late autumn, will charge at the least provocation. I am an authority on this subject since I have been treed twice by these largest land mammals of North America. Likewise be alert when trying to get closeups of such creatures as bison, elk, javelinas, and even sluggish-looking bull seals.

CAMERA AND ACCESSORIES

The camera equipment necessary for mammal photography is identical to that needed for birds (see pages 18-23). I repeat that no one camera will do everything. Some are better suited for certain types of work. Ask any five photographers exhibiting prize-winning wild-mammal shots which camera to use and you may get five different answers.

Single-lens reflex cameras fitted with telephoto or long-focal-length lenses are best suited for stalking large diurnal game or working with the camera in a blind. Last-minute checking of focus, depth of field, background, pose, and composition demonstrates the tremendous advantages offered by the reflex camera. No matter how good the range finder and the viewer on other types of cameras, you cannot be sure of these essential points when working fast, especially under trying conditions. The single-lens reflex is stressed because all parallax problems are eliminated. For working on timid, suspicious subjects at close range, a camera which operates silently is preferable. The noise of the shutter or mirror in some reflex and focal-plane cameras often frightens away nervous mammals with the first exposure.

Press or view cameras with light-lens synchronization are more convenient for flashing nocturnal mammals, and for any mammal photography—day or night—done by remote control. In this type of work the large-size films are preferable, since they allow ample space if the subject is not centered. This space permits later cropping for good composition.

Some photographers prefer 35 mm negatives and color transparencies. Miniature cameras are smaller and lighter and the film decidedly cheaper. Their greatest drawback is the small size of the film, which requires meticulous handling at all times if scratches, fingerprints, and dust spots are not to ruin future enlargements. The single-lens reflex-type miniature coupled with a long-focal-length lens is especially adaptable for many kinds of work. The shutter sound is so soft on most 35 mm cameras that it does not frighten the average mammal. Even when flash is used the camera can be kept in the blind and the lamps set outside as near to the subject as you wish. With electronic flash you can take picture after picture without leaving your blind.

Naturally, the more carefully selected equipment you have, the more versatile your outfit will be. But remember there is a limit to what you can carry in the field without undue fatigue. Do not become a gadget collector.

STALKING

Daylight Stalking

Stalking small mammals in daylight is virtually a waste of time, since you must approach very close to obtain a satisfactorily large image and you will be detected long before you are anywhere near enough. No sport is more exciting, however, than stalking large species. Whereas in most bird photography it is advisable to approach in full view, in large-mammal work it is generally better to keep out of sight. Birds have such keen eyes that they will see you whether you try to hide or not. Unlike the sharp-eyed birds, many mammals have relatively poor eyesight and rely chiefly on acute hearing and a keen sense of smell to warn them of approaching danger.

An upwind approach with the sun at your back is most satisfactory. When working on such creatures as moose, use a slow, steady approach. Each time the animal submerges its head in the water to feed, move forward. Each time it raises his head to breathe, "freeze." If it scrutinizes the edge of the pond, remain perfectly still. As long as you are downwind and fairly well concealed, the chances are you will be undetected. Never forget that mammals have extremely keen hearing. Take every precaution to approach as silently as possible. Avoid unnecessary and, especially, sudden movements. By means of this technique I often have edged within 100 feet of a large bull moose. At such distances I also check my surroundings for the nearest tree that will permit rapid ascent if necessary.

A similar type of stalking can be done by canoe or skiff, but unless the cover is sufficient you will probably be detected long before reaching the 150-foot mark. Success is more likely if you camouflage the bow with dense branches, leaving an opening just large enough to observe and photograph easily. The techniques of approach are similar to those used when afoot. Learn to anticipate the instant the mammal will raise its head. At this point hold the paddle in "frozen" position and keep the boat as steady as waters permit.

In some areas where mammals are protected the year round, they may lose their distrust of man and permit close approach—particularly if you are in a canoe or skiff. The mammals soon grow accustomed to fishermen and realize they mean no harm. In such situations you should approach in full view. Hiding and crouching only tend to arouse suspicion. Do not stare directly at the subject. Pretend your main object is fishing. By a slow, casual approach you often can get as near to some prize as you wish. Sometimes a mammal is so unconcerned it will not assume a striking pose. Then a whistle or loud hum will make the creature stand erect and alert, revealing its full beauty to be captured on the film. Never try to guide your canoe or skiff between the feeding mammal and the shoreline. Even the most confiding moose or deer will become suspicious and depart if it sees its nearest exit to safety about to be blocked.

Carefully study each situation and try to determine in advance the point from which you would prefer to take the picture. It is useless to spend hours stalking a mammal only to wind up in a position where vegetation between you and the subject makes a satisfactory picture impossible. Likewise, sun shining directly into the lens is ruinous.

Some photographers have dressed in furs and antlered head-gear to resemble the creatures they are stalking. I doubt if this attire fools the mammal. If it helps at all, it is in arousing curiosity. Many mammals have deep curiosity and often will stand still or even approach to get a better view of something that attracts their interest. Many hunters know that by sitting still in concealment and periodically flipping a handkerchief into view, they can sometimes draw deer, antelope, and even elk to see what is happening. In fact, I have used this trick, while sitting on a long ocean jetty, to obtain pictures of normally un-approachable diving ducks.

Antelope, mountain goats, bighorn sheep, and other mammals frequenting wide-open areas seldom can be stalked successfully. You must rely on your knowledge of the mammal's habits to approach it. Success is generally commensurate with your breadth of experience. Some mammals in open range or park country have become so accustomed to seeing horses or even jeeps that a photographer can approach closely with one of these conveyances. Be prepared, however, to take your picture from horseback or from the jeep as soon as you come to a halt. Never dismount, for the subjects will then run off.

You may notice that each time you ride into a valley toward antelope, they rush to a particular ridge and travel along that to other feeding grounds. This observation can be used to advan-tage. The next time, station yourself along that ridge out of sight at the most desirable post. Then have your companion ride into the valley and edge the herd to the desired spot. A large part of the fun in nature photography is learning the tricks of the trade. The only satisfactory way to learn is to go afield and have the experiences. Each experience, even the most frustrating disappointment, increases chances of future success. You will discover quickly that, whereas a species shows certain dominating characteristics, each mammal is an individual. One deer or moose may be unsuspicious or even confiding, the next exceedingly shy and unapproachable.

Use of Camera in Stalking

In stalking, the use of a reflex-type camera is virtually essential, for up to the moment of exposure it permits you to check for satisfactory image size, critically sharp focus, pleasing background, and the best composition to capture the feeling of the situation. With a nonreflex camera these essentials are difficult to determine precisely. This is especially true since the use of a long-focal-length lens or telephoto is usually necessary if a large image of the mammal is to be obtained.

With a long-focal-length lens on a miniature camera a tripod is desirable, although good sharp pictures are possible if you remain calm and steady and rely on a gunstock mount or remember to brace your camera firmly. With a 4 x 5 hand-held Graflex I regularly use a 17-inch lens successfully. It is necessary to hold the camera firmly to avoid blurring. I wish to emphasize this point, as it is natural to grow excited or tense when reaching a hard-earned goal. Even a photographer who knows all the fundamentals may concentrate more on snapping pictures than using sound judgment and remembering well-established precautions.

Have the camera as nearly ready as possible before your stalk begins. Take a general light reading and set your speed and aperture accordingly. Estimate the maximum distance at which you will try for a picture, and fix your camera for that distance. Be sure the lens cap is off, black slide pulled, and lens shade and filter in place. Leave as few manipulations as possible for the last minute. Sometimes you may have only one shot, and you must be ready to take advantage of that single split-second opportunity. In good game country I always carry my camera open and ready for operation whether I am traveling by car, canoe, or afoot.

In this type of work where split-second decisions are often necessary, complete familiarity with the camera is imperative. Before embarking on such operations a beginner who uses a nonreflex camera should practice estimating distances, checking each guess with his range finder. No matter which camera is used, he should practice estimating light conditions, checking with his light meter to see if his judgment is good. Thus, when the inevitable situation arises where use of a range finder or light meter is impossible, chance of success is greater.

The advantage of having a companion drive the car or paddle the canoe on such operations is obvious. The cameraman can give his undivided attention to the photographic problems. Generally you want a large image of the main subject. However, if you decide to take some distant shots, be particularly careful to compose your picture to make it striking; try to include beautiful reflections, stirring snow-capped peaks, or any other landscape feature that will contribute a mood of peace, wildness, solitude, or whatever you believe will give most feeling to the picture.

If the mammal is running, the same rules apply as those recommended for birds in flight. Remember that it is much easier to stop motion if the mammal is coming toward rather than parallel to the plane of the film. Use as fast a speed as light conditions permit. When possible, shoot in the direction in which your shadow falls; this position automatically prevents sun from shining into the lens. Learn to swing your camera evenly with the moving subject, releasing the shutter as you continue to follow through. If this is done correctly the mammal will be perfectly sharp and stand out against the blurred background. A background blurring serves to emphasize the movement of the subject.

Stalking at Night

Stalking at night is best done by canoe or skiff because you can move smoothly and silently. The use of a strong jacking lamp, a flashlight used to spot and temporarily blind the subject, is essential. Dark nights are preferable. They not only prevent fogging if the lens is left open, but they offer better cover and assure a more blinding effect from the jacking lamp. I have found this technique superior for larger mammals, but it has occasionally given me amazing closeups of small species, for instance, a beaver on its dam or a raccoon knee deep in water.

In this type of work the reflex camera so superior in daylight stalking offers no advantage. The jacking light is generally too dim to permit last-minute critical focusing and composition. In fact, the difficulty of reliable light-shutter synchronization in many reflex cameras is a disadvantage.

Generally it is better to determine in advance the distance at which you will try for a picture and lock the camera firmly at that distance. Use two photoflash lights, one on each side of the camera, not only for superior light output, but for better over-all illumination. With synchronized equipment the speed and aperture used will depend on the type of film, brilliancy of flash, distance of subject, color of surroundings, and background. Beginners should make test shots in advance to determine the best combination for their equipment. If an open flash is used, a small aperture is preferable because it diminishes the chances of fogging by extraneous light. Fogging can be prevented, of course, by using a lens cap until the minute of exposure. But this offers an additional hazard, for you may forget to remove the cap when the exciting all-absorbing moment arrives.

The camera must be mounted firmly in the bow of the canoe or skiff and locked in a position that will insure good framing if the bow is pointed directly at the subject. All preliminary work should be done before night comes. Once darkness settles it is almost impossible to aim the camera and flash reflectors correctly, and it is difficult to check distance setting, lens aperture, and desired speed.

Once the photographic equipment has been arranged and thoroughly checked, stalking can begin with the dark. It is better to have a companion handle the canoe or skiff while you give undivided attention to jacking the subject and manipulating the camera. Of course, operations should be slow and silent. Once the jacking lamp has picked up the subject, you must keep the light directly in its eyes right up to the moment of exposure. If the light is allowed to wander even for a second, the mammal will undoubtedly spot your craft and flee. Success will depend heavily on your companion. He must know how to handle your craft smoothly and silently. He must be able to judge correctly the distance at which you plan to flash so he can come to a halt at that point and hold the boat absolutely still to prevent blurring of the picture. It will be his responsibility also to point the bow directly at the mammal to insure satisfactory centering. Your major task will be to jack correctly and avoid being trigger-happy. Remain calm and set off the flash at the proper time. Wait for the right moment, but do not get too tense or wait too long and lose your opportunity.

After you have mastered the technique of stalking and have photographed successfully at night, you can mount two complete separate camera outfits on the bow. One will get the subject standing erect. The second, if operated immediately after the initial flash, will catch the startled mammal leaping to safety. The faster the speed of film used, the easier it will be to get clear, brightly illuminated shots with great depth of field. Rapid improvements are being made in electronic flash outfits, but at present they are useless in this type of work, for the light is not sufficient to illuminate subjects so far away.

WAYS OF ATTRACTING MAMMALS

Preliminary explorations of an area may reveal that mammals regularly use certain trails, feeding grounds, or water holes. Take advantage of every opportunity. Bears gathering along salmon streams, beavers gnawing down trees or mending breaks in dams, raccoons coming to a garbage pit, and deer after windfall apples all offer chances for good pictures.

Furthermore, you can create attractions with salt licks, artificial pools, spilled grain, heaped acorns, chunks of meat or fish, honey-coated stumps, fruit, and a great assortment of other feeding stations. I have taken many pictures of small mammals at regular backyard feeding stations and baths established primarily for birds. Advice for the construction of these is given in the section on bird photography (pages 43-46). For large mammals good-sized, natural-looking water holes may be created. These are especially successful in arid places where water is at a premium.

Once mammals come regularly to a given area there are three major ways of obtaining pictures. The photographer may set up a well-camouflaged blind, hide within, and use a reflex camera and long-focal-length lens to make the desired shot. He may set his camera on a tripod or on a brace firmly attached to a tree trunk and release the shutter from a distance by remote control. Or he may devise a system whereby the mammal trips the shutter and takes its own picture.

USE OF BLIND

The discussion on use of blinds and blind construction in the section on bird photography (pages 28-40) gives the fundamentals. There are, however, a few differences in techniques for working on mammals. First, since mammals have so keen a sense of smell and rely on it to a great extent to warn them of danger, be sure to notice the direction of the wind on the day

of photography and set the blind downwind from the spot where
you expect the mammals to come. At the same time give consideration to the position of the sun, for it is generally, though
not always, better to avoid back or side lighting. This is particularly true in color photography. Second, camouflage the
blind thoroughly, because many mammals will avoid a human
structure, especially when it first appears on the scene. One can
camouflage beautifully with surrounding material, or even build
the entire blind from branches, bushes, grasses, and reeds. Make
it look like part of the natural landscape.

At feeding stations or water holes where blinds have been
used for some length of time, most mammals will see the blind
and scent the occupant, but they will learn no harm is intended.
Then you can disregard precautions of camouflage and downwind position. At such places you can build a blind de luxe
with every comfort.

If conditions permit you to place a blind wherever you wish,
bear in mind that in our latitude of the Northern Hemisphere
the sun at noon is directly south. Consequently for midday
work the lens opening should face north, for morning west,
for afternoon east. Always check backgrounds in advance and
avoid all fences, buildings, bridges, paved roads, railroad tracks,
and other objects that could detract from the beauty of the
picture.

The most used and most publicized blind for wild-mammal
photography is the one at the Arizona-Sonora Desert Museum,
about fourteen miles west of Tucson. This blind, a building
twelve feet long by four feet wide, overlooks a small prepared
water hole eleven feet away. Inside, the floor and lower walls
are completely carpeted to deaden the sound of moving feet
and equipment. Comfortable chairs enable the photographers
to relax while awaiting the arrival of subjects. The front of
the blind has four windows, permitting four photographers to
work simultaneously, and its outside wall is covered with re-

flectors for photoflash bulbs. Four of these are synchronized to go off at once, giving an open or time exposure of 1/50 of a second. A 15-watt lamp burning continually illuminates the pool sufficiently to allow the cameramen to choose striking poses. The mammals—including mule deer, peccaries, coyotes, and ring-tailed cats coming to this water hole from the surrounding wilderness of Tucson Mountain Park—have become accustomed to the light. Actually they become nervous when it is turned off or burns out.

Although it was only established in 1954, reservations for use of this blind have been received from every state in the Union and from several foreign countries. The best times there are from April to June and October to December, when natural wilderness water holes are normally dry. Reservations should be made well in advance with the Museum. The directors of this institution deserve high praise for their foresight in establishing such a unique photographic attraction.

Using Camera in Blind

When photographing from a blind, set the camera on a sturdy tripod with a smoothly working, tilting-swivel head. This enables you to have the camera completely ready for any opportunity and you can relax until the very moment your subject appears on the scene. It is humanly impossible to hold a camera in a rigid position for any length of time. Moreover, each additional movement when the subject appears decreases chances of success. Insofar as feasible, determine in advance the approximate spot you wish the mammal to stand and focus on this place. Unless flash will be the main source of light, enabling you to follow a well-established formula, use your light meter, decide on the speed-aperture combination, and adjust your camera accordingly. Check periodically to determine whether changing light conditions demand opening or closing the aperture.

If subsequent events force you to swing your camera in a

different direction and refocus, move slowly and cautiously. Try to make these moves as the mammal turns its head away or bends to feed or drink. If the subject looks in your direction, "freeze" and give it time to lose its suspicion. Check your composition and focus up to the last instant. Wait for the mammal to assume an alert, striking, or interesting pose before releasing the shutter. Assume that each exposure will be your last chance.

When you are working with the camera in the blind, flash presents problems. Naturally, the reflectors and bulbs must be outside. These showy objects not only frighten most mammals, unless the setup has been in operation for a long time, but after each exposure removal of the bulbs and substitution of new ones are necessary. Some persons have suggested keeping the blind near enough to the flashheads so you can make the change without leaving the hideaway. This is useless, for you must reach out to make the adjustments, and any mammal will spot your actions and be frightened. Moreover, use of a long-focal-length lens may enable you to be quite far from the subject. Then it is advisable to use long extensions and place your lamps as near to the place of photography as possible to obtain maximum brilliancy. In such situations electronic flash is far superior to bulbs. It not only assures freezing of all action, but since no bulbs have to be changed you can take picture after picture without showing yourself. Again, however, be sure to have a long extension and a switch which permits you to turn your flash outfit on and off with each exposure; otherwise all energy will quickly drain from the outfit.

Remote Control from Blind

Remote-control photography is recommended only when close-up blind work is impossible, or the use of flash with a short-focal-length lens is imperative. It is satisfactory only when you are quite sure of the spot the mammal will pause. The camera must be fastened to a rigid tripod or convenient support. Focus

8. A Red Squirrel flashed by remote control as it drinks from pool outside a Maine cabin.

9. The Raccoon hesitates as it catches scent of the photographer hidden in a blind near a garbage pit.

10. Reflex camera records two Finback Whales surfacing near a boat off the Maine coast.

11. The photographer's soft whistle makes this White-tailed Deer turn its head for the desired pose.

12. An Eastern Chipmunk on a stone wall is flashed by remote control.

13. At this moment the photographer was more frightened than the Bison!

14. An Armadillo unsuspectingly walks past a bird photographer's blind
set near a Texas pool.

on the point where you expect the mammal to stop, using a printed sign if necessary to check for absolute sharpness. Once the camera is aimed, focused, and locked in place it will be up to the mammal to get in position. If you have any doubts about this position, allow ample surroundings. Later, superfluous material can be cropped for better composition.

With or without flash, an electric cable stretching from a switch in your blind or hiding place to the solenoid release on the camera is desirable. This permits instantaneous exposure at the moment you decide you want a special pose. If you do not have an electrical release and plan to use a long thread, be sure it is dull, inconspicuously colored, and as taut as possible.

In remote-control work, usually only one exposure may be made each time a subject comes. You will have to leave your hiding place to change film, recock the shutter, and in flash work replace the bulbs. Again, if electronic flash is used you must be able to turn it on and off from your hiding place with each exposure.

I have used the remote-control system mostly at feeding stations, drinking pools, nests, dens, and burrows. In such setups the readjustment required after each exposure generally frightens the subject off only momentarily and it returns as soon as I have re-entered the hide. Here too, a companion can be of tremendous help. He can appear after each flash, make any necessary adjustments, and then walk away. This is less frightening to timid mammals than the photographer's sudden emergence from the blind.

If this technique is used at night, arrangements must be made for a small light to illuminate the spot where the mammal is to come. This is the only way to determine when the subject is in the desired spot and pleasantly posed. At night it is even more mandatory that you carefully organize the material in your blind so that you can quickly get what you need without fumbling around in the dark.

SUBJECT TAKES OWN PICTURE

Anyone with slight mechanical ability can arrange a system wherein a subject takes its own picture. The only advantage of this technique is that the photographer does not have to be present. He can work on something else or sleep soundly while some nocturnal creature sets off the flash. Many unusual pictures of shy, seldom-seen mammals may be taken in this way. The disadvantages, however, are many. Only one picture is obtained at a time, generally only one a night. Except in the wildest areas, a dog or cat is likely to pass first and trip the shutter, or an unscrupulous person may steal the equipment. Moreover, the pose of the mammal is purely a matter of luck and a large percentage of the exposures will be unattractive or useless. Unless careful provisions are made for protection, the equipment may be damaged by an unexpected shower, or even by heavy dew if the camera is left out night after night.

The shutter may be released by a mammal walking into the trip line or tugging at bait to which the trip line is attached. You must mount your camera on a firm support. Focus on the selected spot and use precise judgment in placing the trip cord or the bait, making sure the mammal will be in the field of the camera and in focus at the moment of exposure. The distance from the camera to the trip spot or bait, of course, will depend on the size of the subject anticipated at a given situation.

As in all operations requiring use of a thread, be sure it is dull in color so it will be unnoticed by the mammal as well as inconspicuous in the picture. Be sure it is taut. This will insure that the film is exposed at the right moment and there will be no jarring. The thread should be sufficiently strong to release the shutter, yet a section at least should be weak enough to break after the film has been exposed if additional pressure is applied. This will prevent the camera from being upset or damaged. It is not pleasant to find that a coyote has bounded off with the bait in his mouth, pulling the camera, tripod, and flash behind!

For added assurance that the camera will not be jerked over, pass the thread through a screw eye fastened on a tripod leg or through a peg anchored in the ground directly beneath the camera release. Thus the pull will be downward not sideways.

Those with mechanical ability will have fun designing foolproof methods to insure instantaneous but gentle release of the shutter. Simple electric circuits which are completed the instant a mammal·steps or pulls on a lever are the most satisfactory.

If such circuits are not feasible in your case, the simple tripline technique will prove quite satisfactory. With large mammals the trip line may be stretched taut from the shutter release (with flash, the solenoid release), down through the screw eye on the tripod leg and across the trail, and fastened to a tree, peg, or bait. Pressure from a mammal will release the shutter. A tiny hook at the camera end of the trip line will simplify fastening it to any kind of release.

For small mammals whose tug is relatively weak, some device for strengthening the force of the pull is advisable. A simple system is to fasten a mousetrap securely on the side of the tripod leg, and to pass one thread from the bait to the trap's bait lever and a second thread from the trap spring to the camera release. I again emphasize that the thread leading to the camera release must be taut to avoid a sudden jar. A loose connection will jerk the camera and often blur the picture. Some readjustments of the trap spring are generally necessary for maximum efficiency.

As usual in all flash operations, two lamps are advantageous, not only for stronger illumination, but for superior over-all coverage, better modeling, and elimination of harsh, unattractive shadows. The use of electronic flash guarantees that the fastest action will be arrested on the film. But, as I pointed out before, until improvements are made for concentrating the light on a distant subject, this action-freezing light is only satisfactory for small mammals when the lampheads can be placed close to the subject.

Flash work, day or night, in most instances produces a black or almost black background. This is particularly good for nocturnal mammals, as it emphasizes their preference for night. However, some branches or characteristic bushes in focus and framing the scene will add beauty to the picture, especially when you are using color. For diurnal mammals a lighted background may be obtained by making sure close vegetation is directly in back of the subject. When working on small, relatively bold diurnal subjects, place your feeder or bath in front of a branch, rock, or log. A more complete discussion of background problems will be found in the chapter on bird photography (pages 50-51).

ETHICS IN MAMMAL PHOTOGRAPHY

As in wild-bird photography, certain codes are accepted and practiced by virtually all photographers of wild mammals. First and foremost, no mammal must be endangered by the photographer's activities. No picture, no matter how striking, is worth sacrificing the life of the subject. If a deer is frightened to the middle of a lake, do not circle around and around the bewildered creature and drive it to exhaustion. If a tiny fawn is discovered nestled in a fern bed, do not handle it or disarrange the surroundings so much as to increase chances of its detection by predators after you leave.

No real wildlife photographer would use mounted specimens and try to pass them off as wildlife shots. Unless a special sequence is needed for an important educational motion-picture reel, it is inexcusable to stage a combat or predation scene by releasing pets or captive animals at the opportune time. Under no conditions should the result be presented as a lucky one-in-a-million wildlife picture. Once the public realizes you have misrepresented the facts on one occasion, it will automatically question the authenticity of any subsequent pictures bearing your name. Most people naturally assume that a wildlife picture presents an animal free to move as it pleases. In a suburban yard or a national park much of the creature's timidity and suspicion may be gone, but it has a choice of its whereabouts and actions.

Photographs of pets or captured mammals, labeled as such, have their place and use. But such pictures deliberately presented as actual wildlife shots suggest deception. I have admired many beautiful pictures of pets and zoo animals. Photographs by Ylla and others will remain as masterpieces of this type of photography. A collection of such pictures can be of great satisfaction and use, but they should be labeled as zoo, pet, or captive shots.[1]

I once heard a photographer say: "Why take hours or weeks to obtain a picture of a wild animal when similar shots can be obtained in half an hour by using a pet or captive individual?" Another even said: "This is not a sport with me. It is a bread-and-butter proposition and I do not care how I get the pictures." If these photographers openly state their methods and do not present their products as true wildlife pictures, there can be no criticism.

Yet virtually any mammal can be photographed in the wild if the cameraman has imagination and determination. Even a tiny meadow mouse may be enticed out of its runway by placing bait at an opening day after day. As shy and wily a creature as a fox may be lured to a convenient feeding station or water hole, or into taking its own picture on a country trail. A photograph of a wild mole may seem extremely difficult to get, but with sufficient planning and patience one can be flashed as it thrusts its way to the surface.

There is a challenge in seeking pictures of almost unapproachable wild mammals. They are shy, alert, fast-moving, and unpredictable. Matching wits with them gives this type of photography unsurpassed attraction and enjoyment if you have a sporting sense and a love of adventure and the outdoors.

[1] For those interested in this type of work I recommend *A Guide to Photography of Animals* by Samuel Dunton (New York: Greenberg, 1956). The superb staff photographer of the New York Zoological Society here discusses all the tricks for photographing pets as well as animals in cages and large natural-looking enclosures.

AMPHIBIANS AND REPTILES

by Charles E. Mohr

FEW fields of nature have as much to offer the aspiring cameraman or the adventurous naturalist as photographing the cold-blooded reptiles and amphibians. The study of these two groups or classes of backboned animals, called *herpetology,* has been the portal through which thousands of young people have been led to a lifelong interest in the out-of-doors.

Any teacher or camp counselor can attest to the magic power of a live snake to bring a bored or inattentive group to instant alertness. Any hike leader knows the excitement caused by an unexpected encounter with a leaping frog, a slithering serpent, or a scurrying lizard.

The more serious naturalist may use photographs of reptiles and amphibians for several purposes: as a useful substitute for preserved specimens when collecting is impossible or undesirable, as a valuable supplement to scientific collections, or as a graphic, indisputable record of behavior seldom described or witnessed.

For the advanced photographer, herpetology offers a challenging field of operations. Countless types of pictures of these wildlife forms are still waiting to be made. The reptiles and amphibians can serve as subjects for slides and prints which attract fresh attention and awards no longer to be won with photographs of more conventional subjects.

SCOPE OF THE FIELD

Most amphibians neither look nor behave much like reptiles, though salamanders are sometimes mistaken for their reptilian counterparts, the lizards. Any good series of pictures would clearly distinguish the smooth skins typical of most salamanders and frogs, and the somewhat warty skins of toads, in contrast to the scaly coats of snakes and lizards, the leathery skins of alligators and crocodiles, and the armorlike covering of turtles.

The eager cameraman must go hunting amphibians at night if he would photograph them performing most actively and naturally, while most reptiles are strictly creatures of the daytime world. The thin-skinned salamanders and frogs are likely to dry up and die in the matter of minutes if fully exposed to the direct rays of the sun. Many reptiles, on the other hand, habitually bask in the sun.

In some cases, however, the extremes of desert or midsummer temperatures cause certain snakes and lizards to adopt nocturnal existence. Finding such reptiles is largely a matter of luck, but frogs and toads will obligingly lead the photographer to their haunts. Every suitable night during the breeding season the males proclaim their presence at ponds and waterholes, and the voiceless female frogs beam their course to the calls of the males.

As with birds, the sounds produced by each amphibian vocalist are distinct enough to permit positive identification of the species. Among the reptiles the only vocal performance of note is the occasional bellowing of the bull alligator, a sound few naturalists get to hear.

With such a wide variety of subject matter within this field the photographer can look forward to many months of camera hunting—during all but the winter months, when freezing weather finds every reptile and most amphibians out of reach in subterranean hibernating quarters. Of course, there are still pictures to be taken in more tropical climates, and there are other picture possibilities which will be mentioned later in this chapter.

REQUIREMENTS

As in every other field of photography, the finest pictures are taken by those with the best camera technique and the most knowledge of the subject. Since a high score in both fields is discouragingly rare, one obvious solution is *teamwork*.

With a naturalist to decide where and when to look for pictures and knowing what behavior is significant, a capable photographer with suitable equipment can take pictures of more than passing interest. Some of his shots may well be unique—"firsts" of some unusual species, or of meaningful behavior.

Lacking a field companion of such talents, the photographer new to the field is well advised to consult in person or write to herpetologists in the nearest museum or zoo. Often the expert can give suggestions specific enough for the photographer to discover the animals desired and to have a good idea of the kinds of pictures which would be most worth attempting. A lot can be learned from books, of course, and there are many fine new ones in this field.

The better trained the naturalist, the higher are his standards of nature photography and the greater is his disdain for "nature-faking." His greatest satisfaction is derived from the picture which shows the subject unrestrained, under completely natural conditions.

If the animal must be maneuvered into camera range or into a less cluttered setting, two considerations are paramount: the safety of the subject and the authentic naturalness of the pose and setting.

No conscientious nature photographer will knowingly injure a specimen in order to get a picture. Nor will he pit together in "combat" species which would not normally be found in a predator-prey relationship. He attempts to record on film what animals normally do, not what might be dreamed up by a poorly informed person whose imagination runs wild.

PICTURE STANDARDS

Keeping pace with improvements in cameras, accessories, and film is the growing awareness of what qualities go into a good picture, regardless of the subject:

1. *Good Composition.* The negative should be well filled and the subject placed so that there is "room for action." That is, there should be more space in front of an animal than behind it. If the subject is too small on the negative, it will not make a good enlargement, or a large-enough image if projected.

2. *Good Detail.* Focus should be absolutely sharp on the animal pictured. If a head-on view, it should be sharply in focus at least as far back as the eyes. Enlargements to 8 x 10 size should be possible without excessive graininess. Detail should be good both in shadow and in highlight areas. Lighting necessary for adequate illumination will be discussed later.

3. *Suitable Background.* Whether or not to have the background in focus is debatable and will have to be determined by the purpose of the picture, the angle of view, and the lens equipment employed. What is even more important is being alert to extraneous material behind, around, or in front of the subject. It may be a dried blade of grass, a dead leaf, a shiny rock, or any one of a dozen objects that photograph lighter than the main subject and therefore become distracting elements in the finished print or slide. Or it may be a dark branch or stem which seems to rise out of the animal's·body. So many otherwise fine pictures have been ruined by extraneous detail that I cannot emphasize too much the need for constant alertness to this hazard.

Sometimes the photographer is aware of these background defects, or of grasses or branches partially obscuring the subject, but hesitates to move them because he may frighten the animal into flight. Most photographers take at least one shot for "in-

surance"; then, with great care, attempt to maneuver the offending object out of the way.

At times a log, rock, slab of bark, or perhaps a large leaf or a
fern frond can be slowly lowered into position behind the animal
so as to provide a natural but less cluttered background. If the
animal being photographed is a poisonous snake, it is wise to
have someone else distract the snake while the extraneous objects are removed or the backgrounds rearranged—always with a
knowledge of the distance a snake can strike.

One author goes so far as to say that no photographer working
alone should ever attempt to photograph a poisonous snake. I am
inclined to agree, remembering a time in Florida when I was
focusing on a coral snake scarcely a yard away. As I peered into
the ground glass the snake suddenly disappeared from the field
of view. By the time I located it, it had passed beneath my tripod
only inches from my feet.

CAMERAS AND EQUIPMENT

The size of the subject and the degree of its wariness are the
major factors influencing the choice of camera and lenses.

Scarcely any subjects among the amphibians, save an army of
migrating salamanders or a swarm of little toads emerging from
a pond to a terrestrial existence, offer much opportunity to the
photographer equipped only with a box camera or other inex-
pensive type devoid of supplementary lens equipment. Even
when fitted with a "portrait" lens recommended for extreme
close-ups of flowers and other still-life subjects, results are dis-
appointing because the animals generally will not tolerate an
approach within the necessary ten to twenty inches.

Many reptiles are much larger, of course, and good pictures of
alligators, marine turtles and tortoises, and the bigger snakes and
lizards can be made with almost any type of camera.

Twin-lens reflex cameras can be used effectively in photographing large reptiles which are not too wary to approach somewhat

closely or can be photographed at close range from a blind. The advantage of this popular type of camera is that it permits a brilliant full-size view of the subject until the moment the picture is taken.

This is possible because the upper, viewing lens is used at full opening or aperture even though the lower, taking lens may be stopped down until it lets in so little light that it is difficult to focus and frame the picture through it, let alone judge the best moment to snap it. Since the viewing-lens image is clearly visible on the ground glass, a tripod is less essential than with single-lens reflex cameras where the image becomes dim when the lens aperture is reduced.

Single-lens reflex cameras are the most popular for all-round nature photography. Since they accommodate a wide variety of lenses, from wide-angle to 400 to 600 mm or even longer telephotos, these cameras are extremely versatile. The image seen on the ground glass, or through a prism, is exactly what the camera will record. This is true regardless of the lens or number of extension tubes on the camera. Since many lenses now have click stops which enable the photographer to count the stops, or have a ring permitting presetting of the desired aperture, the actual stopping down can be done in a split second before the exposure is made. In this way the chief objection—poor visibility through the lens—is overcome.

Although the standard lens—approximately 50 mm—on most 35 mm single-lens reflex cameras can be used with extension tubes for extreme close-up work on plants and many other stationary nature subjects, amphibians and reptiles rarely tolerate the close approach these lenses require. Unfortunately this objection applies also to the remarkable new lenses which focus from infinity to a few inches by means of a deep-set helical focusing mount.

Telephoto or long-focus lenses make possible a large negative image at a greater distance from the subject. Most useful for photographing reptiles and amphibians is the 135 mm lens. Mechanically and optically good lenses of this length are now available for most 35 mm cameras for as little as $40.

Range-finder type 35 mm cameras accommodate coupled lenses up to 135 mm, and the latest models of the more expensive makes have much improved visibility in focusing and framing the picture. Nevertheless, through-the-lens viewing generally is more satisfactory, so some device for turning the range-finder camera into a ground-glass-focusing camera is often used. This modification can be accomplished by a patented device known as a Speed-o-copy, or by a reflex housing mounted between the camera and the lens. Several brands are on the market.

Second in importance to the camera and the 135 mm lens for photography in this field is the bellows focusing device, which permits extremely rapid changes in the degree of enlargement. While photographing a wild, unrestrained copperhead recently with this combination, I shot first from ten feet, then quickly from six, four, and finally, with a companion monopolizing the snake's attention, from about 24 inches. As the camera was moved closer, the bellows was racked out farther. A life-size 1 to 1 reproduction is possible with this lens at a distance of approximately 11 inches from the subject; but with the copperhead, I was satisfied with a negative image somewhat smaller than life size.

The versatility of 35 mm cameras, their economy in film and processing costs, and their suitability for color photography account for their popularity in the nature field. The vast majority of 35 mm pictures are color slides made for projection.

In my opinion, the value of such equipment for black-and-white photography has generally been underrated. For anyone who has mastered the techniques of fine-grain developing, the new films provide a medium for superior work. It is unfortunately true that much commercial developing of 35 mm film is unreliable, and that commercial enlarging is expensive and often mediocre or worse. But the photographer who makes a practice of doing his own developing and enlarging can confidently expect semi-matte prints of salon quality in sizes up to 11 x 14 or larger. Incidentally, camera club membership and participation in club and salon competitions are of great value for improving one's technique and awareness.

While it is true that fine black-and-white prints can sometimes be made from color transparencies, I personally prefer to shoot any important subject both in color and black and white. This is easy when a reflex housing, with or without bellows, is being employed, and two cameras are available. I find that I can change from the color camera to the one loaded with panchromatic film in from ten to fifteen seconds, simply unscrewing one camera and replacing it with the second. (The tripod head is secured to the reflex housing, not to the camera.) Generally this involves a slight change in lens opening, or the black-and-white camera can be preset at a faster shutter speed. One of the great advantages of the miniature cameras over the larger sizes is, of course, their simplicity and speed of operation.

A larger *view camera* is the choice of quite a few older or more advanced nature photographers who seek consistently high-quality negatives or large-size color transparencies with a view to use in publications. If the camera is to be used out of doors, a film size not larger than 4 x 5 is preferred. Naturally, film cost is much greater than with 35 mm size. Pictures are more carefully taken, as a rule, and in much less abundance.

Double- or triple-extension bellows are useful for accommodating lenses of various focal lengths, though some view or press cameras can be equipped with extension tubes to achieve the same effect. Some of the most expensive cameras have adjustable fronts and backs, making it possible to bring a greater amount of the subject into focus and to compose the picture on the ground glass without moving the camera itself. This feature is especially handy when photographing a coiled snake which would be hard to get fully in focus with any other type of camera.

Whatever the camera used, the important consideration is the photographer's ability to handle it easily, almost automatically. With absorbing and active subjects there is little hope for the cameraman who fumbles over unfamiilar adjustments.

Tripods

Although both reflex cameras and range-finder cameras equipped with reflex housing may be hand-held for moderate close-ups, serious problems will be encountered. For example, the limited depth of field makes it hard to keep the focus critically sharp when operating without a tripod. Unless you can brace yourself or the camera against the ground, a tree, rock, fence, or other solid object, it is better to use a tripod when photographing small subjects.

Another reason for using a tripod is to avoid wear and tear on the photographer. Considerable time may be involved in waiting for the subject to strike a characteristic pose, or to commence or resume some activity, such as a turtle or snake laying eggs. A tripod is important, too, when a sequence of close-ups is being made, for with the hand-held camera it is often harder to keep the subject precisely located in the field.

In addition to a standard-sized tripod, preferably of the elevator type, a miniature tripod is essential for many kinds of pictures. I prefer a small but sturdy type with adjustable legs, one which places the camera two to eight inches above the ground. Some of the more expensive large tripods have means of attaching a camera to a bar which can be lowered close to the ground. The "worm's-eye views" of trilling toads, basking turtles, and curious salamanders made possible by low camera angle and prone position of the photographer provide many of the most startling and interesting pictures.

The tripod head deserves a word of comment. Unless it is positive in its locking action, yet easily loosened and readjusted, it will cause the loss of many pictures. It is better to have a large reliable pan head on a small tripod than to fret over a head that is too small to get at and adjust easily when a quick change is necessary.

Flash Equipment

New models of flash equipment appear with such frequency that there seems to be little point in describing it here except in general terms. Almost all of it can be grouped in three categories:

Flashgun Powered by Battery. Power supplied by comparatively short-lived dry batteries of flashlight-size fires magnesium-packed flashbulbs. Midget bulbs usually are satisfactory for black-and-white photography at the close ranges involved, the somewhat larger miniature bulbs for color. Flashbulbs must, of course, be discarded after a single firing.

Flashgun Powered by Battery Capacitator. This equipment does not differ from the previous type except that the power output is more consistent, with the battery lasting approximately a year.

Electronic Flash Unit. The powerful built-in capacitator of a "strobe" or speedlight is discharged through an electronic flash-lamp. This eliminates the need for changing bulbs. Since the lamphead is good for at least 10,000 exposures, this represents economy as well as convenience for the photographer who takes a lot of pictures.

Out-of-doors flash may be necessary when natural lighting is inadequate or uneven. It may be used as a fill-in to illuminate shadows, reproducing detail which otherwise would be lost.

For indoor photography of amphibians and reptiles, flash is indispensable. Not only does flash permit pictures of fast action, as already noted, but also it is easy on the subjects. Thin, moist-skinned salamanders, and many of the frogs, cannot stand much exposure under floodlight or spotlights. Even reptiles, though they are often sun-loving creatures, have limited tolerance of high temperatures.

Snakes that are abroad by day can survive heat of 100 to 105 degrees, but if their body temperatures rise above 110 degrees death is almost certain. Nocturnal species are less tolerant of high temperatures; 100 degrees is likely to be lethal, and 90 degrees for aquatic species.

When amphibians or reptiles are transported in closed containers, such as cans or jars, special care must be taken to keep them cool. They are best transported at temperatures of 40 to 60 degrees; and if the animals are to be kept for any length of time without feeding, they may be left in a refrigerator, but not near the freezing compartment.

The body temperature of these cold-blooded, or *poikilothermic,* creatures is approximately the same as that of their surroundings; their metabolism is reduced as the temperature drops, but more so among reptiles than among the amphibians, which may breed in waters only a few degrees above freezing.

Some photographers recommend cooling off reptiles in a refrigerator as a preliminary to photographing them. Personally I prefer the more natural poses that a normally active snake or lizard takes after it has had time to get acquainted with its quarters.

Heat is to be recommended in one type of reptile photography, that of turtles. Often a timid turtle will pull in its head and refuse to stick it out again. The most effective kind of persuasion is a photoflood or infrared lamp, which generally induces the reptile to take a man-made sun bath.

I have used a diametrically different scheme to make salamanders comfortable. When I use spotlights while focusing on the cold-loving amphibians, I drip ice water upon them or spray a cold mist on them with an atomizer.

Reptiles are best confined in a glass-topped aquarium or glass-sided cage for close-up photography. Salamanders may be photographed in a moss-lined tray or an unglazed pottery dish, provided someone is nearby to keep a constant watch on the sub-

15. Male Toad in midst of his mating song, a melodious trill. Toads sometimes sing in daytime but more commonly after dark.

16. After 24 hours the salamander egg masses will have swelled to full size. It will take about one month for the eggs to hatch. Here they are lifted out of the water. Some related salamanders lay eggs free of any branches or other vegetation.

17. Embryo Red-backed Salamanders hang in a grape-like cluster in a little cavity beneath a rock. Each egg is about a quarter-inch in diameter. The transparent envelopes reveal a large amount of yolk in each egg. Prominent dark spots are the eyes.

18. Quizzical pair of Long-tailed Salamanders peer out of a crevice in their cavern home.

19. Rare albino salamander was photographed but not collected because a long term study of the salamander population of the cave was under way. A normal salamander is seen on the left.

20. Portrait of a Copperhead showing the characteristic eliptical pupil and the pit located between the eye and nostril, which contains sensory cells that can detect the presence of a warm-blooded animal, the snake's prey.

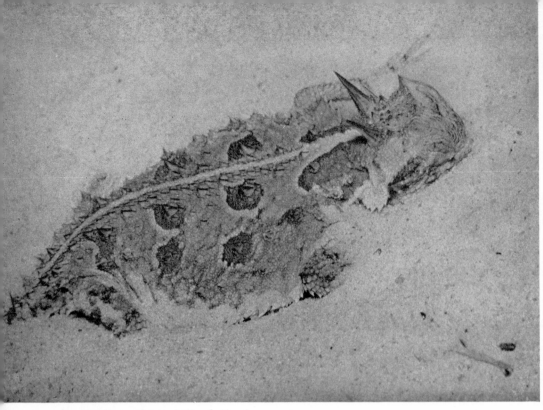

21. A Texas Horned Toad digs in.

22. Roofed Turtle, a species from Southeast Asia, eyeing the landscape of the New York Zoological Garden.

ject. Some species of salamanders can leap several inches and will unhesitatingly launch themselves into mid-air in attempts to escape. They may expire in a few minutes if they fall to the floor or crawl into some other dry situation.

My favorite method of "table-top" photography is to place my setting—dish, tray, aquarium, or other glass-sided enclosure—on a bridge table. This permits a ground-level view and it also enables the cameraman to shift quickly to one side or another if his subject moves into a pose in either direction.

Perhaps better would be a Lazy Susan, which would permit the whole setting to be turned to take advantage of a variety of poses. Lights could be mounted on the stable portion of the table, so few if any adjustments would have to be made.

It is desirable to have at least two lights on the subject. The closer the camera is to the subject, the greater will be the angle of light incidence (unless a round-the-lens flashtube is used). Consequently, a single light under such conditions throws bad shadows.

HOW TO FIND AMPHIBIANS AND REPTILES

There are two ways of going camera hunting. One is the planned trip. The other might be called the "beachcombing" technique. The broader your photographic interests, the better this latter method works. You can hardly ever go outdoors without finding some natural object of interest. But a great many haphazard nature walks would fail to turn up a single amphibian or reptile. To be successful in this specialized field, thoughtful planning based on some definite information must precede any photographic foray.

Knowing where to go for a particular species usually pays off in picture opportunities. For example, Florida is the place to find wild alligators; but since they were hunted until a few years ago, when protective laws were passed, they are wary. In the Everglades National Park, however, they have enjoyed protection for much longer. The ranger-naturalists can generally predict where in the Park big alligators are to be found. One particularly fearless six-foot 'gator can be seen regularly from Anhinga Trail, a boardwalk which starts near the park headquarters and winds through the swamp for several hundred feet. Egrets, herons, and many other spectacular birds can be seen from the boardwalk, but the sight of the solitary big reptile is a high spot of the trip for many observers.

Snakes, as a rule, are hard to find. In rocky country, where they are known to den up in the fall, a sharp-eyed explorer may find them by the dozen. Often the location of snake dens can be learned from old-timers in the area. Some species will be virtually invisible among the variegated fallen leaves as the snakes assemble for hibernation each fall. That is why it may be better to go snake hunting in spring when the reptiles are emerging from their underground wintering quarters and can be more easily detected.

Incidentally, I have read of a number of these dens or "hibernacula" opened by accident, revealing scores of intertwined snakes of several species. There are also reports of aggregations of hibernating salamanders numbering in the hundreds. I have never seen a photograph of such an occurrence; it would probably be an important "first."

As snakes scatter from their dens in spring, they become more difficult to find and harder to photograph. Most often they are found in or close to stone walls; under bark and slabs, especially around abandoned sawmills; or under boards, pieces of tin, or tar paper.

Rarely does one get a chance to photograph a snake on the first encounter. But by returning to the spot where snakes were seen the persistent cameraman may successfully stalk his wary prey. Snakes are usually warned by the heavy, earthshaking footfalls of the approaching hiker or photographer. Such vibrations are detected easily because the reptile's whole body is likely to be in contact with the ground. But when approached stealthily, a snake probably will lift its head from the ground, extend its delicate, forked tongue in an effort to pick up clues as to the nature of the approaching object, and stand its ground. The picture possibilities are good if one prowls quietly, avoiding quick movements which would alarm the snake.

Turtles are easy enough to find if you search for them along the edges of ponds and quiet streams. Here they bask in the warm sun for hours. These sun bathers are more alert than they appear. They have picked logs and stumps projecting out over the water, and at the first hint of danger they slip silently into the water and remain submerged.

Later the turtles will slowly lift their nostrils above the surface (they are air breathers) and will make sure the coast is clear before climbing out of the water. Good photographs can be made from a blind or from a slowly moving canoe. With a telephoto lens of 200 mm or longer, interesting groups and individual turtles can be shot in a variety of characteristic, sometime humorous, poses.

Away from water you may have a hard time discovering a turtle, even though box and wood turtles are common. Several times in late summer I have happened upon a box turtle and moved it to a spot where mushrooms were growing. Sometimes the timid reptile would slowly open its shell, notice the mushrooms, and proceed to take a few bites. Often, however, the presence of the tripod and camera a few feet away would seem to alarm it. At such times a turtle can be a cantankerous creature. More than once I have spent an hour waiting in vain for one of these uncooperative reptiles to make a move, but some sunny summer day I'll get the shot I want.

On the other hand, a rainy day or, better yet, a damp spring evening following a heavy shower is just what the camera fan needs if he is looking for frogs or toads to photograph. As I have said, they are not hard to find, and once you learn how to approach them, you should not have any trouble getting pictures.

It is a good idea first to study the lay of the land by daylight. Do not tramp casually over unfamiliar terrain in the night. You might wind up entangled in a barbed wire fence or face to face with a gun-toting farmer.

It is better to scout the most promising meadows, swamps, and woodland ponds by day, decide where you can safely and legally park your car, where the landowner resides so you can get permission for your expedition, and just where the sounds in the night might have been coming from.

Actually, at the height of the breeding season frogs and toads seem to observe a 24-hour day, calling almost continuously if the temperature and humidity are right. But your chance of photographing during daylight hours is slight. Almost invariably the calls cease as you approach, long before you can spot any of the singers. They see you first.

On a few occasions, in daylight with thunderstorms approaching, I have found toads absorbed in their singing and oblivious to my presence. But I much prefer the shots made at night.

Part of the fun of hunting with a camera after dark is the element of surprise. You never know what you will meet, from a startled deer or a prowling raccoon to a barn owl peering quizzically at you from a hollow tree.

Or you yourself may suddenly be impaled by the probing beam of a prowl car's spotlight. When that happened to me one spring night near Buffalo, New York, I headed for the police car to explain what I was doing. I had captured a couple of the tiny swamp tree frogs and had them in a jar. But when I exhibited them to the doubting cops, I had trouble convincing them either that such tiny creatures could make such a racket or that I would be able to take pictures of them out there in the swamp. As it turned out, my pictures were good and I later had a chance to show the same policemen a big blow-up of one of the frogs snapped at the moment of his supreme vocal effort.

For trying your hand at the same sort of thing, I recommend that you start with toads. The nights will be warmer. That may seem a hazardous prediction, but it is really a rather safe one because the amphibian chorus operates on a recognizable timetable based on temperature. Once the ground has thawed in late winter and the first rains have come, swamp tree frogs *(Pseudacris)* may start calling when the temperature is as low as 28 or 29 degrees. Spring peepers *(Hyla)* will begin to tune up at about 33 degrees. Toads demand higher temperatures.

Nights as cold as the low 30's don't produce enough calling to make it worth while to try for pictures. The frogs are too easily discouraged by your presence. But within a couple of weeks some misty night will come along when the temperature reaches 50 degrees. That is the time to get into your hip boots and wade out into the wet meadows or along roadside ditches.

A spotlight worn on your head will leave your hands free for your camera and tripod, and with the light in that position you will be able to see reflections from the eyes of spiders, frogs, and other creatures.

It is a great help to have a companion on your expedition. Often you can locate a frog best by triangulation. Here is how it works. Stand some distance apart with your lights turned off. Then when you think you have located the source of the nearest frog song, turn on and point your flashlights in that direction. Very often the singer will be just about where the beams converge. Usually that spot is farther away than you calculated.

It takes some patience to find a frog that measures less than an inch in body length. With a little practice you can become expert at spotting them. The swamp tree frog's call is a "click-click-click." He has three parallel stripes down his back and usually sits at the water's edge or perches on a partially submerged leaf or twig. Spring peepers are miniature tree frogs with an *x* on their back. The single note of a peeper is a short whistle. In the distance it sounds remarkably like sleighbells. Often peepers will climb a blade of grass or onto a low branch of some shrub.

Don't be discouraged when the swamp becomes silent as you approach. If you will stand perfectly still some frogs in the distance will resume calling. Then nearer ones will gain courage until finally all the frogs have rejoined the chorus.

Spring peepers are easily encouraged, I have learned. Sometimes after I have maneuvered into position about two feet from a peeper I quickly focus on him, using a 135 mm lens with either a reflex housing or a focaslide attachment on my 35 mm camera. Then, satisfied with focus and composition on the ground glass, I stop down the lens and pause, waiting for him to resume calling. If he remains silent I try to persuade him to "sing" by imitating his short whistle. Most of the time it works.

Startled by the nearness of a possible rival, I suppose, he will puff up his throat and give forth with the familiar "beep, beep, beep." Once he hits his vocal stride he will keep it up no matter how many times my strobe flashes; no matter how many flashbulbs I use.

Once in a New Jersey swamp I set out to count the number of consecutive calls a peeper might give. Several frogs persisted for 100 calls or more, but the champion went to 1600, stopping only when a rattletrap car came clanking down a nearby lane. I was able to get a series of slides showing the same frog: first while sitting silent, his throat not extended; another when completely puffed up, his throat expanded into a bubble far larger than his head; and a third when he relaxed between calls. Since this quiet interval lasted only one second, his throat pouch did not have time to be completely withdrawn; his "bubble" even then was larger than his head.

At this in-between stage his body was a little more slender than normal. When calling the loudest every bit of air must have been pushed out of his lungs into his throat pouch, for he looked downright skinny—a condition I wasn't conscious of until I studied my pictures. It is surprising how often photographs reveal details of which the cameraman was unaware when the picture was taken.

Watching a frog perform, you may be puzzled by the fact that he sings with his mouth shut. It is the passage of air back and forth from the lungs to the bubblelike vocal sac that vibrates the vocal cords. The air in the distended pouch causes it to function as a sounding board.

In the whole field of nature photography I have found no more exciting adventure than this business of catching frogs and toads in their moments of vocal glory. It is not always easy. Most frustrating are species like the common wood frog that spend their time floating on the surface of the water and calling while afloat. I have found it next to impossible to wade so stealthily that I could approach close enough to set up my tripod on the uneven, debris-cluttered, and muddy pond bottom, then spot them in my headlamp long enough to focus.

A hundred times they have edged away or have submerged just as I was ready to shoot. On the rare occasions when they remained in the field of view they have been stubbornly silent. Perhaps you will have better luck than I have had.

The wood frog and a number of related species in the genus *Rana* give the cameraman only a split second to catch their calling performance. Their vocal pouches extend along the side of the jaw and are expanded for only a moment.

The most outstanding series of frog and toad pictures yet published were those made by Dr. Arthur A. Allen for *National Geographic Magazine* while recording songs for his superb "Voices of the Night." This record makes it easy for anyone to learn to identify the calls of the frogs and toads of eastern North America.

You are certain to get pictures of salon quality if you concentrate on toads. For one thing, they are much bigger than the spring peepers and swamp tree frogs. They come out later in the spring when it is more comfortable to be abroad at night, and they are easy to locate and approach. Moreover, they are generally only a foot or two offshore, in water up to an inch or two in depth.

If you get down to ground, or water, level you will be in the right position to make some really imposing pictures when the hopeful males sit up quite erect and burst into their musical trill. Unlike the short almost explosive notes of the *Ranas,* the melodious trill of *Bufo,* the toad, may last half a minute or more.

A whole story may be brought out in your pictures. First a band of singing males by the water's edge. Then a close-up of the biggest bubble-blowing male. Don't miss the approach of the not-so-timid female. Later, offshore, you may be able to photograph a mated, clasped pair as the larger female lays long strings of eggs, several thousand of them. Put a few of these eggs in a quart, or better, a gallon, jar of pond water so that you can take them back and record their development in a series of aquarium shots. But if you put too many of the eggs into a container, they will quickly use up all the oxygen in the water and die.

The advent of summer ushers in a new cast of amphibians. Of special interest to the photographer are the bullfrogs and the tree toads. Listen for the deep bass "jug o'rum" of the big bullfrogs down by the water's edge and the staccato woodpeckerlike rattle of the tree-dwelling *Hylas.* They will lead you to exceptional picture opportunities.

Not only are tree toads notable for their ability to match the color of their surroundings, be they off-white, tan, green, or gray, but the big disks or pads on the tips of their fingers and toes enable them to perform acrobatic feats so engrossing that the watcher may have trouble concentrating on picture taking.

Tree frogs (they are not really toads) also blow oversize bubbles with their expandable throat pouches, and finally come down out of the trees to mate and lay their eggs in the nearest pond or swimming pool.

I have spent hundreds of hours afield with frogs and toads and have many pictures to show for my efforts. Almost as much time has been consumed searching for salamanders, with far thinner results, for the "spring lizards," as the country children know these long-tailed amphibians, are silent. More knowledge of their way of life is necessary to get first-rate pictures of these subjects.

The same early spring rains that set off the first frogs seem to trigger the mass migration of the big terrestrial salamanders, the *Ambystomas*. Most of them are robust, measure six to twelve inches in length, and are black or dark gray in color, some with bold spots or patches of yellow or silver.

Aroused from winter-long hibernation by the warm rains, these salamanders work their way to the surface of the ground and then at night head unerringly to the nearest flooded field or woodland pond. Arriving a few days in advance, the swarming males deposit minute spermataphores, pyramids of gelatine topped with a sac of germ cells.

When the fatter females arrive a few nights later, a gyrating *Liebesspiel* begins—an exciting courtship performance that will test the mettle of the most skillful and persistent photographer. The drama is concluded by the females settling over the sperm-filled capsules, then moving off to selected spots where newly fertilized eggs are laid en masse. Just once, in the mountains of central Pennsylvania, I witnessed this communal egg-laying of a species I have long studied, the Jefferson's salamander, named for the naturalist President.

There was no time for a tripod, no chance to put on a focaslide attachment. I simply set the lens at 3½ feet, the shutter on bulb, and moved in until the range finder showed the salamanders to be in focus. All this was done in the beam of a flashlight held between my knees as I stood alone in the shallow water of a woodland pond. Then, turning my legs to swing the light out of the way, I opened the shutter, set off my hand-held flashgun, and closed the shutter. The resulting picture, while not technically perfect, is unique.

Before the advent of really dependable flash guns for cameras equipped with focal-plane shutters, open-flash photography provided a simple and effective way of getting nighttime pictures of nature subjects. I still use it occasionally when taking pictures in caves, especially when several other photographers want to "ride the flash."

Caves, incidentally, offer year-round picture opportunities. The uniform temperature and the humid atmosphere to be found in many of them provide ideal living conditions for moist-skinned salamanders. In some cases the long-tailed creatures move into caves to escape from the heat and dryness of midsummer, in other cases to spend an active winter. There is no need to hibernate in a cave; freezing conditions are not encountered there.

Cave-dwelling salamanders are found in greatest variety in the South, in the limestone areas stretching from Tennessee to the Ozarks of Missouri, and in Texas. Twice while studying and photographing salamanders in caves I have found species new to science, and twice I have come across salamander eggs of types not previously described. Naturally, pictures of such discoveries have scientific as well as personal interest.

The eggs of one of these salamanders were laid in a shallow underground stream, the others in tiny crypts in a tall travertine column in a commercial cave. The owner of a Kentucky cave led me to the spot where several of the small zigzag-striped salamanders could be seen, each guarding a little cluster of from three to five white eggs, about a quarter inch in diameter. Each salamander occupied its own cubicle, though three of them could be seen in the space of a few inches.

How was I going to photograph the guardian parent partly coiled around the eggs? The crevice was only an inch wide, the occupant at least an inch back, and my camera, mounted on my tallest tripod, pretty completely blocked the opening.

Since there was a power line in the cave I decided to take advantage of it. I chose a spotlight in preference to flash. By utilizing a small old 100-watt slide projector, I could send a finger of light deep into the crevice and so avoid extreme over-exposure of the out-of-focus portals of the nesting chamber. An exposure of a half second did the trick; the salamander obliged by holding perfectly still.

This zigzag-striped salamander reminded me of its close relative, the very common "red-back" that inhabits our woodlands. There it finds protection from heat and drought by living under stones, and under or inside decaying logs. A few times in early summer I have found and photographed them in these situations and have gotten down to their level with a miniature tripod.

Since they guard their eggs constantly for about two months, these woodland salamanders offer a fairly long season for the persistent naturalist-photographer. Look in *moist* spots for the abundant "dusky." About midsummer this species hollows out a cavity under a stone and lays its eggs there. As late as September I have found "nests," sometimes having as many as thirty eggs with well-developed embryos showing clearly through their transparent envelopes.

Let me add a word of caution. If you start turning over logs and stones in search of salamanders, be sure to replace everything exactly as you found it. Putting a log or stone only part-way back into the depression from which you pulled it results in this small but important habitat drying out until it becomes desert-like and uninhabitable by the host of organisms that live there.

USE OF CAPTIVE ANIMALS

Now and then the salamanders, frogs, lizards, and small snakes you find will impress you with their extreme interest as photographic subjects, but time or circumstances may severely limit your opportunities for getting good pictures. Why not bring them back and photograph them under more favorable conditions? This is perfectly legitimate from the naturalist's viewpoint, as long as you follow the rules of the game:

1. Let the welfare of your captive be the most important consideration. Learn how to keep amphibians moist without drown-

ing them. Most reptiles require drier quarters. Different species have different requirements. Offer them appropriate food, but keep alert for uneaten food that may spoil and contaminate the water or the vegetation or soil in terrarium or cage. There are a number of books on pets and captive animals that will give specific directions for keeping them successfully.

2. When you prepare photographic settings for your captives, let your artistry be directed toward creating a realistic, natural-looking environment. The more closely you've observed the animal in the wild, and the more fully you understand its habits and needs, the better photographic job you can do.

3. Let the activity pictured be genuine. Let it represent behavior you have witnessed on your expeditions but could not manage to photograph in the field. You may, of course, observe and photograph things in an aquarium, such as egg-laying or the stalking and capture of prey, that you might never observe out-of-doors for lack of time.

4. Never state that posed shots of captive specimens were taken under natural conditions. This is not meant to discourage "controlled" indoor-picture setups. They have their place and may result in pictures that are both useful and artistically satisfying. They may at times be more convincing and more revealing of the special environment of a particular creature than the best picture that can be taken under difficult field conditions. But the challenge of the really fine wild shot is always greater, the satisfaction more lasting.

In working with captive animals you may become absorbed in certain problems, such as the lightninglike action of a toad's tongue as it picks off a live insect, or the spectacular leap of a tree toad which covers a space twenty times its own length. Can you photograph such fast action? Of course, with speedlights that produce flashes of very short duration. Even the strike of a rattlesnake has been caught on film. The main problem is in keeping the action within a narrowly prescribed plane.

To photograph *Bufo*, the toad, picking up a mealworm placed in front of the camera, one photographer set the stage on a copper plate. As the toad's moist tongue flipped out against the worm and contacted the copper surface, an electrical circuit was completed, setting off the flash and taking the picture.

Audubon lecturer Robert C. Hermes once had a "stable" of tree frogs and learned that by holding a frog in his hand and using his fingers as "blinders" he could so restrict the frog's view that he could control the direction of its leap. Many of his pictures of frogs "frozen" in mid-air reveal details never seen or known before because the leap is faster than the eye. Another photographer, W. T. Davidson, dangled a butterfly above and in front of a bullfrog and shot it in the middle of its upward leap, a striking color protograph which *Natural History* magazine chose for one of its covers.

The belief that a rattler could strike fast enough to intercept a pistol shot, or that it was quick enough to dodge a bullet, was once widely accepted in the West. Walker Van Riper, of the Denver Museum of Natural History, succeeded in measuring the speed at which a big prairie rattlesnake strikes. He did it photographically, using electronic flash equipment which was set off when the snake's lunge cut across an electric-eye beam. The interruption actuated a relay which controlled two high-speed flashes, one going off instantly, the other after a delay of 20 to 30 milliseconds. By including a timing device and a ruler in the background of the picture it was easy to calculate the distance the snake's head covered in the elapsed time.

When results were computed, Van Riper discovered that the average speed of the strike was eight feet per second—less than six miles per hour! A boxer can strike much faster; a golfer's hands travel five times as fast in swinging a golf club.

While it is true that most animal movements are relatively slow—the fastest snake travels at about four miles per hour—they are still fast when you are trying to photograph them from a distance of only a foot or two. It takes light brighter than sun-light to record such movements on film. Flash is the answer.

Sometimes a white reflecting surface, or a mirror, may be used to cast enough light into the shadow to bring out detail there. As a rule a second light source, on an extension or activated by a slave unit, is needed. In many situations where a background is involved, a third light source will prove beneficial, filling in shadows and building the tone or color of the background to a degree comparable to the foreground.

Captive specimens in zoos also may provide good picture possi-bilities, but under somewhat more limiting circumstances. You will have no opportunity to arrange the setting, but with patience and an eye for camera angles you may get some unusual pictures. Some of the world's most interesting reptiles come from distant lands—the giant Komodo "dragon"; the primitive tuatara lizard, with its third "eye"; the true chameleon, with its free-wheeling eyes and telescopic tongue; the enormous reticulated python; the venomous Gila monster, now becoming rare; and other snakes and lizards, frogs and toads, of many descriptions.

In zoo photography you occasionally have bars to contend with, though most large reptiles (other than snakes) are con-fined in open pits. More often the animals will be behind glass that produces bothersome reflections. If you avoid shooting at right angles to the glass and keep your flash on or close to the camera, you can generally avoid reflections. A pocket flashlight will enable you to experiment and discover in advance how the light will bounce. This is absolutely essential if you use a second light source, for it is difficult to avoid a reflection in the glass when a supplementary light is involved.

SAFETY FIRST

I have urged that specimens being photographed be given the utmost consideration. A word should also be said about the photographer's well-being when he handles reptiles. Any medium-sized or large snake can inflict a painful wound with its multiple rows of sharp needlelike teeth. Usually a snake *lifted* gently (*not* held tightly around the neck or pinned down with a "snake stick") and lightly restrained will not become alarmed. To be on the safe side, some handlers prefer to wear old leather dress gloves when working with nonvenomous snakes. Obviously, such gloves do not give adequate protection against the much longer fangs of a poisonous snake, and heavy leather gloves are dangerously clumsy to wear.

Unfortunately, deadly reptiles have an irresistable fascination for many adolescent boys and occasional adults. To handle any poisonous snake is to take considerable risk—a foolhardy one unless you have had a great deal of experience with reptiles. Many zoo workers and other professional snake handlers have been bitten by venomous snakes and a number have died from the effects of the bites. There are so many other challenging fields in herpetology that you can well afford to limit your contacts with poisonous reptiles to specimens in the zoo.

RESULTS

By following the basic tips given in this chapter and constantly expanding your knowledge of your subjects, you should be able to take pictures of many types—some artistic enough to hang in a pictorial salon; others of special scientific interest; many that will illustrate universal nature themes, such as camouflage, natural variation, and predation; some that show minute detail not readily seen by the casual observer. And you may get the perfect shot now and then that is good enough to meet the exacting demands of textbook or magazine publishers. But whether you use your prints and slides for photographic competition, for teaching or lecturing, for illustrating articles or books, or just for your own enjoyment, the new and exciting experiences you have in getting them will make this kind of camera hunting truly memorable and satisfying.

INSECTS

by Edward S. Ross

MORE than three fourths of the kinds of living things are insects. The effect of this imposing percentage is magnified by the great abundance of individuals and the often drastic changes in appearance which occur during the life development of most insect species. For example, each kind of butterfly not only has winged adult beauty but also curiously shaped and sculptured eggs, several distinct caterpillar stages, and a strange chrysalis.

Such diversity has long been an intriguing challenge to students of insect biology and classification. Now, with recently available photographic equipment, the fabulous insect world offers increased and almost unlimited opportunity to the camera-bearing hunter.

Such "hunters" find particular satisfaction because so many insect species have never before been recorded on film and photography affords the best, if not the only satisfactory, way of communicating knowledge of a living insect's appearance and habits to a wide audience. A good photograph from nature has value at all educational levels, from that of research analysis at one extreme to that of delighting the small child at the other. In the case of the larger, more easily observed animals, photography plays a lesser role because so many such subjects have been frequently photographed, or can be seen in the field or zoo with no more special optical aid than ordinary field glasses or binoculars. In a sense, the insect photographer carries a film-loaded microscope in the form of a camera.

Another appealing aspect of insect photography is that the diversity of potential subjects makes it possible for even the most modest local field trip to be a high adventure. One never can predict what miniature drama, awaits encounter and filming behind the next grass clump, stone, or leaf in the grassroot jungle along one's path. An insect photographer need never return home without having made many exposures, and the suspense continues on through to the viewing of the processed film and prints.

THE PROBLEMS

Before discussing the problems and difficulties inherent to insect photography, we might state the ideal objective we are striving to attain. This ideal is the same as that of any good nature photographer, whether his subjects be birds, mammals, reptiles, or insects. We are simply trying to record on film the natural appearance, posture, and habits of some creature in its natural environment. Even the best nature photographers find that they must at times compromise on the environment factor. But, in general, one should strive to encounter the subject on its home grounds rather than bring the subject *to* a place where it can be most conveniently photographed. In short, one must ideally use his equipment for hunting and not entirely as laboratory or studio instruments.

Although insect photography is about as old as photography itself, *true* insect hunting with a camera is definitely a new opportunity. Insects are small, often active and elusive, and thus much of the past effort to photograph them was limited by the inadequacy of available equipment. These earlier efforts were largely confined to naturally sluggish or inactive species, or to those recently emerged from a cocoon or chrysalis. These would be most likely to stay put long enough for the photographer to set up his tripod, frame and focus on ground glass, insert his film, and, at long last, finally click his shutter.

Often the more active insects had to be killed and posed in what seemed to be the proper posture. Even within the last decade there have been articles describing these methods in which animals are merely used as objects of still-life photography. To this day there are photographers who can "live" with pictures they have taken by temporarily quieting the active insect with a whiff of ether or chloroform. Still others, perhaps in a fit of desperation, nearly freeze, or, as they say, "temperature control," the active little ceatures with a shot of CO_2 or confinement in a refrigerator or portable icebox. Needless to say, such methods cannot be classed as wildlife photography or hunting with a camera.

Rather recently, photographic equipment has become available in great variety and price ranges, rendering such "nature faking" inexcusable. Combined with the all-important desire to excel, and to work hard with great patience, these relatively new tools enable one to accomplish wonders in the candid portrayal of the insect world. Even the most difficult form of insect photography—insects in flight—can become almost routine.

CAMERAS AND EQUIPMENT

Choice of Camera

The first requirement of the camera for the insect subject, or any other close-up, for that matter, is an ability to frame and focus through the picture-taking lens while being able to make an exposure at any moment.

Such desirable attributes are embodied in the modern single-lens reflex cameras available in a number of brands, chiefly imported. The most versatile of these has interchangeable eye-level (prismatic) and waist-level viewers. The latter is highly desirable for the many ground-level shots, the former for most other levels.

One other essential requirement of a camera for insect hunting is synchronization of the shutter with flash—particularly electronic flash.

The choice of camera size, whether 35 mm or the 2¼ x 2¼ size, is debatable. Arguments in favor of the latter emphasize with justification that it is the best size for the many larger insects, such as butterflies and grasshoppers, which can be photographed at or near natural size. The larger negative is also desirable for still bigger subjects—frogs, birds, mammals, and the usual pictorial assignments. Also negative grain and other picture-processing problems are less critical than with 35 mm.

Favoring 35 mm is the fact that many insects are very small and must be magnified to take full advantage of even the small 35 mm film area. In such cases, when larger film sizes are used, one either wastes vast film surface or he enlarges the image so much that other difficulties arise, such as loss of depth of field. In a sense, one of the great dilemmas in close-up photography is the need to keep the image size as small as possible to gain depth of field, but yet large enough to resolve detail. Another factor is that nature photography is largely a game of chance— the more shots one takes (with due discretion), the more likely he is to produce the occasional truly outstanding picture. The lower cost of film for 35 mm cameras makes it economically possible to shoot more freely and to vary the exposure by means of the lens aperture or flashlamp position. The 36-exposure capacity of the smaller cameras also reduces the need for frequent reloading. There are many other advantages as well: the 35 mm color transparency is almost a standard for projection, the cameras are light and more maneuverable, and some brands offer interchangeable viewers. In short, as an owner of both sizes of reflex cameras, I find 35 mm most useful and versatile for insect photography. With proper exposures and careful film and print processing, I experience little grain or resolution difficulty with the small negatives.

Those wishing to undertake insect photography with cameras having indirect viewers for framing and focusing must if possible introduce a reflex housing between camera body and lens to gain many of the advantages of the true single-lens reflex camera. The sliding-back focusing devices for such cameras represent a return to the Dark Ages of tripod-rooted close-up nature photography.

Another way of taking close-ups without benefit of a single-lens reflex is to use a focal frame—four divergent framing wires projected forward from the lens. Their tips should outline the frame and represent the plane of focus of the particular length of extension. Precision focus is out of the question, but these wires, even with single-lens reflex, function as a very useful sport finder for shooting rapidly moving subjects, such as insects in flight. If sufficient tries are made, one is certain to secure an occasional sharply focused picture.

However, if you intend to do much close-up nature photography, by all means start right off with a single-lens reflex camera, or turn in any unsuitable equipment toward its purchase. I will not deny that outstanding insect pictures—even candid ones—can be, and have been, made with other types of cameras. I am merely recommending the single-lens reflex camera as a tool which makes true insect hunting with a camera a routine matter.

Fortunately, the equipment one needs for insect photography, and much of the technique, can be applied to all sorts of close-up subjects, such as spiders, reptiles, and frogs. With special accessories removed, the same cameras can be turned on the full range of common photographic assignments—people, scenery, and the like.

Lenses

Perhaps the most common reaction of the layman to close-up pictures is, "You must have a wonderful lens to magnify the subjects!" Actually, most of my work has been done with the standard, often least expensive, lenses available for my brand of camera. The "magnification" results from the increase of the lens-to-film distance through the use of metal extension tubes or bellows. In black-and-white work, further magnification is possible, of course, by enlarger projection in the darkroom.

Another common question concerns the use of telephoto lenses as a means of avoiding close approaches which often frighten the subject. Although I have a 135 mm telephoto lens, I never use it for close-up work. One reason for this is that I began insect photography with an ordinary 50 mm lens and all of my hard-earned trial-and-error experience in estimating lens apertures and light position is based on the particular lens-to-subject distance resulting from the use of a 50 mm lens. I would rather risk the consequences of closer stalking than lose the advantage of this experience.

Another important factor is that when a telephoto lens is used, more extension is required to produce the desired image size and, worst of all, the flashlamp is farther away from the subject. This means less subject illumination and a need to increase the lens aperture and thereby suffer a loss of depth of field.

Therefore, at least for the beginner, I recommend starting with a standard F 3.5 or F2.8, 50 mm lens of good quality—preferably individually tested for high resolving power. Among the great variety of available lenses, you should choose one having a preset diaphragm ring. This ring enables you to set the aperture in advance, to start focusing wide open, and yet to be able to stop down to a preset aperture without moving the eye from the viewer. This is an advantage in focusing hand-held close-ups under poor light conditions.

Ideally, however, one should be able to approach a subject and frame, focus, and trip the shutter without having to reach forward to stop down the lens in a separate action. In good light you can avoid this problem by merely framing and focusing with the lens stopped down in advance to even as fine an aperture as f/22. This has been my basic technique to date, but it requires excellent eyesight and good trigger timing of the shutter release.

I am now commencing work with one of the new lenses having an automatic diaphragm. Such lenses enable one to focus at all times with the lens wide open. The lens snaps to a preset finer aperture with the same pressure that releases the shutter an instant later. As extension is almost always used in close-up work, it is necessary to use a twin-cable release—one to the diaphragm release and another to the shutter—to gain the advantages of the automatic features. The twin-cable release system, however, brings out new difficulties in the quick exchange of metal extension tubes, additional gadgets in the way, and the gripping of the camera. With special instrumentation I expect to reduce or eliminate these disadvantages.

Another useful type of close-up lens has built-in extension tubes which telescope into an extensively projected lens shade. This makes possible a great range of image size without the use of separate tubes or bellows. As yet, however, such lenses do not have the automatic diaphragm feature. As the focusing light problem is more critical than that of using removable extension tubes, it appears advisable to sacrifice the built-in extension advantage in favor of the automatic diaphragm.

Before leaving the lens subject, I should mention the use of macrophotographic lenses, namely, the Microtessars, Microsummars, etc. These lenses are especially designed for high magnification work. Their need, at least theoretically, arises when the lens-to-subject distance is less than the lens-to-film distance. Although such lenses come in small mounts with a 20 mm thread to screw into the objective mount of a compound microscope, they can be used with camera extension tubes by mounting them in a special disk threaded to screw into the end of an extension tube.

These special lenses are seldom required in field photography, and their need is most frequent for special laboratory projects. Frankly, I cannot detect any difference in resolution between work done with my standard F 2.8 Tessar and my F 4.5 Microtessar.

Extension of Focal Length

Some sort of extension of the lens-to-film distance is required to produce the desired image size. Its amount will depend on the focal length of the lens used—the shorter focal lengths requiring less extension than the longer lenses to produce the same image size.

For field work I much prefer metal or Bakelite tubes rather than bellows, as the tubes are cheaper, more durable, and less bulky. They can be distributed in pockets, and with experience one can soon accurately estimate what lengths to add or subtract for each subject encounter.

In purchasing a set of tubes, make certain that the interior surface is dull black and grooved to break up light reflections. When great lengths of tubing are used (I often use more than six inches), there is increased danger of reflection on even a dull interior surface and this can ruin the picture. The insertion of a roll of black feltlike paper, as used for lining some lens shades, may reduce this problem.

I prefer bellows, often in combination with tubes, for high-magnification work. A tripod is usually required because it is almost impossible to hold critically fine focus when the camera is hand-held. In wandering about the field for subjects, I object to the fragility of bellows. Also, the constant projection of the rack in front of the lens increases the danger of frightening the subject or of contacting and jarring the plant surface on which it may stand.

Illuminating the Subject

With a single-lens reflex camera, a good lens, and a set of extension tubes, you can begin insect photography of a sort. Such was my stock of equipment when I began serious work a few years ago. However, most of the pictures I took in those days have long been discarded because I was not then using supplementary light, namely, flash.

The problem is simple: in close-up photography the light reaching the film is greatly reduced in two ways. First, some is lost when the lens-to-film distance is increased to produce an enlarged image. Second, some is also lost as the lens is stopped down to the fine apertures needed to create depth of field. To overcome this one must reduce the shutter speed to 1/25 of a second or less.

All this means that blurred pictures can be avoided only by holding the camera very steady, usually on a tripod. It is also necessary to have the subject, and the surface upon which it rests, absolutely motionless. Even under the most ideal conditions the resultant pictures are usually inferior because of some unavoidable movement. Added to all this is the fact that one's efforts are confined to but a few commonly photographed sunlit subjects and the use of the tripod restricts the ability of the photographer to take candid pictures.

The obvious answer to this problem is to increase the illumination artificially so that the exposure can be greatly reduced while permitting the use of the smallest possible lens aperture. A floodlight can be used under special circumstances, but a water-cell barrier is almost necessary to protect the subject from intense heat. This disadvantage is coupled with the "leashing" of the photographer's activities to the length of his electric cord.

The next alternative is flashbulbs. However, these increase the cost per picture try, and add to the bulk of things to carry and to dispose of without littering the countryside. I believe flashbulbs should be resorted to only by persons with cameras that do not synchronize with electronic flash.

Electronic flash

The greatest boon to insect photography has been electronic flash, which more than pays for its rather high initial cost in convenience, saving on flashbulb cost and, above all, increased picture quality.

Such flash results from the sudden conduction of electricity through a twisted or coiled glass tube containing the gas xenon. The necessary high voltage is built up in capacitors deriving electricity from batteries or household current. The exposure time is that of the instantaneous flash resulting from the ionization of the xenon, usually less than 1/1000 of a second, rather than the speed of the camera shutter, which is usually set at no less than 1/50 of a second in single-lens reflex cameras.

There is a decided advantage in the quick succession of pictures which can be made without stopping to change bulbs. The light quality closely approaches that of sunlight and no filters are required for black-and-white and daylight color film, indoors or out. Generally, at the small apertures used in combination with extension, only the flash image is recorded on the film. The sun image, recorded at the slow shutter speed, may consist only of streaked highlights—especially those on the wings of insects in movement.

The high acceptance of electronic flash is evidenced by the many brands on the market. One's choice will depend on his pocketbook and the recommendation of a trusted dealer. In addition to a small movable lamphead, the features most to be desired are dependable flashing and easy portability. For closeups great throwing power is unnecessary.

I work with a small unit having a standard lamp. This is kept detached from the power pack and camera so that its position can be varied. I am inclined to avoid the special units which enable the flash tube to encircle the lens, since these must produce too flat a lighting. Even though the subjects are small, the same principles of good lighting apply in insects as in human studio portraiture. The ideal we can never hope to achieve in our field snapshots, but we can at least keep our flashlamp free—not only for angling the light but also for varying our exposures. If there is an art or knack to insect photography, much of it involves the proper play of the electronic flash on the subject.

Miscellaneous Equipment

Tripod. Although true insect hunting with a camera must be candid, hence "freehand," a serious photographer will find many uses for a tripod. There are many insect photographs, such as close-up micro-aquarium shots and records of stages in the life history of species, which can or must be taken from a tripod or similar support in or out of the laboratory or studio. Such support is also essential for holding focus on insects requiring high magnification, such as aphis. The tripod should have a crank-operated shaft for changing the camera level.

Exposure Meter. All photographers ought to have a meter, but I have long since abandoned its use for flashed close-ups. Through trial and error and recorded experiments one should develop an "eye" for exposure. The best work in this field can only be done with flash, and exposure is conditiond by the lens aperture, lamp position, and the reflective quality of the subject and its surroundings. A good instinct for exposure is one of the intangible knacks of close-up work. No two situations are identical and the subjects will not always stay put, or continue their activity, to await the calculations of the more methodical photographer.

Background Cards. A stiff, matte, sky-blue background card is essential for many situations. This should be kept clean and protected in some sort of case. I deplore the use of any other color than that of the sky because blue is the only naturally occurring uniform or continuous color in nature. The intensity of the blue can be varied by the distance the card is placed from the light source. The desired illusion is to have the subject appear to be standing against a sky background, and for this reason great care should be taken to avoid shadows on the card.

Whenever possible, I try to use the chance natural backgrounds of nature, since these can be an important part of our photographic record. However, if the subject is dark, and no natural light background, such as a leaf, is behind it within the "throw" range of the flash to create a correct exposure, the picture is likely to be a failure; for the background will register black and thus will not define the subject. However, in the case of pale or light-margined species, such black backgrounds may prove to be desirable. The effect may be that of night photography, and this may be undesirable in the case of insects known to be active only during the day.

Film. With flash there will be ample light to enable the use of slow, fine-grain, black-and-white films. Whether the film is monochromatic or color, it may prove wise to confine yourself to as few emulsion speeds as possible in order to develop dependable experience in positioning the light and adjusting the lens aperture.

INSECT-FILMING EXPEDITIONS

Every red-blooded person has a gaming instinct in some degree. We are intrigued by activities in which the outcome is unpredictable. Some persons find their outlet in gambling, horse-racing, athletic events, and games of other sorts. A higher level of the gaming spirit is expressed in the form of exploration or the thrills of discovery in the scientific research laboratory. At the very root of all this is the love of the chase or the hunt—that successful coping with the unexpected which must have been a big factor in developing the human intellect.

In photography, therefore, it is not surprising that the greatest sport is to be had in unexpected trailside encounters rather than in the carefully planned photographic projects of the laboratory or studio.

So let us festoon ourselves with the proper "weapons" and go on our first insect-filming field trip, discussing methods as we go along the way.

The reflex camera, free of its case, is suspended from our neck by a sturdy strap. A moderate length of extension tube has been added behind the lens. Extra lengths are distributed in various pockets. A light electronic-flash unit is slung across the shoulder, its strap beneath that of the camera. The flashlamp cord is looped under an arm and across the back of our neck. The proper cord connects the flashlamp to the camera's synchronization plug and we are all set to go.

Anyone who has the purchase price can drape his body with such equipment. From here on out the play of persistence, patience, keen eyesight, knowledge of the subject, in combination with the indefinable "knack," determine the degree of success.

As we walk down the trail the cameraman should take the lead. Like any good insect hunter, his eyes should scan every surface for possible subjects. At times insects will be seen merely sitting or busy with their various activities in specific niches, such as flowers, on leaves, etc. Others will reveal themselves by suddenly leaping, running, or flying and can then be followed to the places where they alight.

When a likely subject is sighted, you should stand motionless until the proper length of extension tube is in place, the lens aperture set, the camera cocked (the shutter speed should constantly be set at 1/25 or 1/50 of a second with electronic flash), and the flash power pack turned on. (When the subject encounter is frequent, this may be kept on for long periods of time.)

Then you should decide on the angle of approach—provided there is a choice. Generally this will be the one presenting the greatest possible subject surface parallel to the plane of the film. Consideration should also be given to level of approach. As a rule it is best to avoid perpendicular views. Instead, strive to shoot at the level of the surface on which the insect stands—in other words, get down to the insect's viewpoint. At times, however, especially for portraits, the three-quarter-front approach is most desirable. Each approach will be determined by the particular environmental circumstances, the form of the species, and the objectives of the photographer.

Having decided on the approach, with due consideration of the effect your shadow may have on the subject's behavior and the focusing light, you slowly close in to range, frame, focus, and click the shutter. The gradual approach is usually best because insects are less alarmed by slow movements.

Focusing is accomplished by moving the whole camera and not by adjusting the lens mount. The greatest depth of field results when you place the prime plane of focus somewhat behind the subject's nearest surface. If you focus on the nearest surface, relatively sharp focus is lost in thin air in front of the subject and the more distant surfaces are likely to be more blurred than they need be. Generally, it is wise to focus on the head of the insect, since this is the center of interest in any insect picture.

The position and angle of the flash is very important. In effect, you hold the sun in your hands and can create any desired lighting effect. Light can become a standardized factor in each particular photographic problem, and thus, with experience, your work is greatly simplified. The proper use of the flash can only be developed by experience. Some may wish to fasten the lamphead on an adjustable bracket attached to the camera. For better or worse I keep mine unattached and, by operating the camera almost solely with the left hand, my right is free to move the light about as the situation seems to require. Usually the right hand partially grips or braces the side of the camera and the lamp plane is very close to that of the lens itself, but angled from above and inward.

Because of the intensity of the flash, f 22 is commonly used on black-and-white shots and f 16 is average for color films with an ASA index rating of 8. As more extension tube is added, the lens and flash lamp move in unison closer to the subject and this more or less compensates for the reduction of image light intensity caused by the lengthening of the focal length. At very high magnification, the lens aperture may be opened to f 11, but seldom more. The whole question of lens aperture and lamp position varies according to the type of flash and film used and the reflective quality of the subject and its immediate surroundings. At first you should experiment, keeping a record of the varied apertures and lighting. There is no substitute for experience or instinct in such matters.

When a very special or rare photographic subject presents itself, even the most experienced photographer should take a series of pictures with varied light and apertures, not only to insure making at least one technically perfect shot but also to increase the odds of recording some interesting activity. Even if I have repeatedly photographed a certain species, I always consider making additional exposures in an effort to top my past coverage of the subject.

PHOTOGRAPHY IN FLOWERS

Flowers and insects are often interdependent. Many kinds of insects tap flowers for energy-giving nectar; others visit them to gather pollen, and the flower benefits by being cross-pollinated. Still other insects are flower eaters and many wait in them, or search them, for insect prey. Thus flowers can be one of the most productive places to photograph insects, and the flower itself can be as interesting an element in the composition as the insect.

The best flowers are those with large simple petals rather than "tweedy" textured bunches of small flowers in a single head. White flowers can be difficult because of their tendency to "bounce" too much of the flash. Often the reflection of color from the flower petals will distort that of the insect.

Among the many subjects to photograph in flowers are butterfly visitors, including close-up portraits depicting tongue action; ambush bugs and crab spiders catching prey; bees and other pollinators. If one flower seems to be attractive to a passing series of visitors, an interesting picture story can be made by photographing the traffic over a given period of time. If the flower sways too much in the wind, it can be made rigid by lashing its stem (just beneath the flower) to a slender wooden or steel stake driven into the ground next to the plant.

INSECTS ON FOLIAGE AND STEMS

Next to flowers, a search of foliage and stems reveals many fine insects. Many insects use leaf surfaces merely as a place to sit, but a great variety of leaf-eating species, such as interesting cater-pillars, will be found. Provision should be made to rear the latter to maturity so that the life-history story can be completed.

It will soon be noted that each kind of plant tends to have its particular set of insects, and these in turn will be prey to many a different species of predator or parasite. For example, the dire hazards in the life of the aphis can fill many rolls of film: parasites pop out of tiny trapdoors in aphis bodies, lady-bird beetles and lacewings—larval and adult—gobble them up, and blind fly maggots consume them in great quantities as they grope about.

GROUND LEVEL

The ground is the level of much insect activity. On such surfaces the camera should be trained as low as possible so that the insects will loom dramatically high. At this level the photog-rapher must creep and crawl, and his work will be greatly eased if his camera has a so-called waist-level viewer so that the photographer's focusing view is perpendicular to the ground surface rather than from behind the camera.

If the tone of the ground is pale, as on alkaline flats and sand, the flash should be used with care to avoid overexposure. Sometimes I use indirect or bounce light to reduce such flare. If the insect stands fairly high, try to hold the light directly over it so that the shadow will be directly beneath. This insures that there will be pale background visible through the legs and this will sharply define the heavily shaded ventral surface of the creature.

In addition to the opportunity to shoot insects merely rest-ing, or using the ground as a surface to walk on, the important ground-level subjects will be the many kinds of wasps, ants, and bees nesting in the soil. When active nest holes are found you can record the various comings and goings of the occupants as well as the activities of their enemies.

Most dramatic are the many digging wasps, each kind carrying or dragging insect or spider prey into the nest holes. For example, *Sphex* wasps bring in caterpillars, sand wasps (*Epibembix*) prey on flies, spider wasps (*Pompilidae*) provision their nests with spiders. None of these stories is complete without photographs of the underground chambers showing what happens to the prey. This leads to depictions of the fascinating life-history stories which inspired some of the greatest entomological literature, notably that of Fabre.

In such excavation work, you must set your camera to one side, but ready for immediate use. Dig a large hole next to the burrow opening. Then, with a trowel, carefully shave away the wall of the hole, exposing first a profile of the entrance shaft or slanted burrow. Eventually, the larval chamber will be found and its contents photographed after you have first made sure that it is free of dirt or sand which fell in during the digging. Here is where artificial light is invaluable, because you cannot depend on sunlight to illuminate such subterranean subjects properly. If you want the full story on the underground life of insects, it may be necessary to excavate scores of nests. Some of the life history can be continued in artificial cells in the laboratory.

MARGINS OF STREAMS, PONDS, AND LAKES

The fresh-water shore is the scene of much insect traffic. Perhaps the first to attract attention are the dragonflies. However, with their great bulging, all-seeing eyes they are about the most unapproachable of insects. As with all insects, the chances of getting within range are greatly increased if they are busy eating or mating, and such activity adds interest to the picture. The problem is greatly increased by the fact that dragonflies so often perch hawklike on high places with a sky background. Such shots will usually be failures unless a blue background card is in place, and this is an almost impossible requirement. Eventually, one can find dragonflies repeatedly perching on a reed or

23. Working at all levels, the insect photographer gets plenty of exercise. A Caterpillar Hunting Wasp may emerge from a hole at any moment and the photographer must hold his focus ready to snap the shutter with perfect timing. (From *Insects Close Up,* courtesy of California Academy of Sciences.)

24. The Caterpillar Hunting Wasp makes a fine study in flight. This one is about to land after having jettisoned in mid-air a load of sand excavated from its burrow. (From *Insects Close Up,* courtesy of California Academy of Sciences.)

25. The success of this picture is due to simple, yet natural surroundings (a smooth, broad leaf), against which an interesting, normal insect activity is clearly defined—a young Assassin Bug sucking the body juices of a tiny wasp. Note that the cast shadow does not merge with that outlining the bug's underside. This desirable effect results from an overhead aim of the flash.

26. The Sand Wasp's larva, fat from a diet of flies, completes its development in a cell deep in the dune. To record these interesting wasp stories, the photographer must make careful excavations of the profile of the nests.

27. Candid close-ups can record the meaning of form and pattern in nature. Here a tropical butterfly rests, in characteristic fashion, upside down on tree bark which it so closely resembles. Often repeated, stealthy approaches are required to get but one shot of such an alert insect.

28. The Snakefly—a relative of the familiar Green Lacewing—stands "kneedeep" in Honeysuckle Aphis serving as its food. The long "tail" is used for inserting eggs in crevices of bark. This interesting form was carefully aligned with the film plane. A background card gives the effect of sky.

29. Long-tongued Bee is an apt name for this glistening, metallic-green tropical beauty. Ordinarily the long tongue is used for sucking nectar from the deep corollas of flowers like orchids, but this bee was tempted by candy-sweetened sputum on a leaf.

twig near the water surface. With this surface as a background, you can set up and wait ready to shoot much as you do in a blind for a bird to return to a nest. In fact, some sort of camouflage like a blind is not a bad idea in coping with this and other wary insect subjects.

In addition to the dragonflies, and their relatives the damselflies, margins of water environments are fine hunting grounds for many other insects—mayflies, caddisflies, stoneflies, etc.—most of which just sit and are thus easy to photograph. As adults they do nothing exciting and the only photographic challenge is securing interesting composition or recording the transformation of such species from their aquatic nymph stage to the adult.

On sandy beaches and dunes much sport will be found. For example, just try to get a good picture of the fleet tiger beetles. The dunes will also be found to be the home of many interesting wasps.

NIGHT PHOTOGRAPHY

Night photography of insects can be one of the most appealing of photographic sports, for you can do some real pioneering in the portrayal of nature. With electronic flash the only problem at night is securing sufficient focusing light. One method is for a companion to locate and illuminate subjects with a large flashlight while the cameraman draws his bead. You can also experiment with the use of a lamp on a hat, as used by miners and cave explorers. Artificial light never will replace sunlight for focusing, but the preset aperture ring will prove useful at night for opening and closing the diaphragm without moving the eye from the viewer. The new automatic lenses, however, are the answer to any such focusing problem in poor light.

At night you can photograph the many insects which are active only then, as well as record the nocturnal resting habits of the diurnal species. Each type of environment, whether it be a meadow on a warm summer evening, a night in the desert, or a trek through a tropical jungle, offers exciting night photography opportunities.

STUDIO INSECT PHOTOGRAPHY

The most valuable and satisfying pictures will be those made candidly in the field. This applies in all types of true-to-life photography, whether the subjects be human or insect. However, insect lives are complex and certain stages are passed in places which cannot be reached or photographed by sole reliance on the freehand, candid method.

For example, a good insect photographer should depict adult butterflies in action in the field, and ideally his pictures should demonstrate not only appearance but also the things that adult butterflies do—sucking nectar, mating, laying eggs, etc. But to insure full coverage of the life history of any species of butterfiy, breeding cages in the studio or laboratory are necessary to record such events as the hatching of eggs; caterpillar stages and the action of transformation (ecdysis), including that of chrysalis formation; and, finally, the very emergence of the adult from the chrysalis. The photographer should also strive to photograph the various wasp and fly parasites of the species concerned.

This rounding out of the pictorial record of an insect's life can be attempted for many species, but the methods of achieving such results involve more ingenuity in rearing insects than in photography. These ways are so diverse that one must refer to the entomological literature for guidance.

In addition to life-history studies, glassed-in colonies of various social insects, such as ants, termites, and observation hives of honeybees and bumblebees, can be maintained.

Special laboratory procedure must also be used for aquatic insects. At times you can photograph these in their natural pools if the water is clear, shallow, and free of surface ripple. But, as with most animals, the best photographic views are to be had at animal level. Although I have had no experience in such specialized photography, I am sure that an ingenious worker could devise various ways of getting his camera down to these levels in the natural water environments. However, the usual method is to have aquaria with thin, clear glass walls and to do the photography in the studio, or immediately adjacent to the body of water.

Water insects can be maintained for varying periods of time in larger aquaria, and for actual photography they can be transferred to smaller narrow containers. For mosquito larvae and pupae I make micro-aquaria out of rectangular microscope-slide coverslips (the type used for tissue sections). If one wishes to show the water line in the picture, these slips should be perfectly aligned and the concave or convex meniscus should be eliminated by filling the micro-aquarium exactly level with the top edges of the glass. This can be adjusted by pipetting in water or by drawing off excess with a corner of a blotter. For such pictures I often use an illuminated diffused background of opal glass.

INSECTS IN FLIGHT

Because it is the most difficult, flight photography is the greatest sporting challenge of insect photography. Most of the commonly used cheaper electronic flash units are fast enough to stop all action except the wings. However, I feel that blurred wings give the pictures more action and life than those made with the high-speed lights. Such stopped-action pictures are most useful as an aid in studying flight dyamics rather than as a means of recording insect flight as it appears to our eyes.

The short depth of field in which insect photographers are confined limits the number of flight situations that may be covered. In general, we must have some predictable flight pattern to work with.

The easiest flying insects to start with are those entering and leaving flowers. One may first make the flower rigid by lashing its stem to a stake. Then set up the camera on a tripod so that at least part of the flower is in one corner of the frame and as much open space as possible remains. A blue background card should be in place because the real sky will record black due to underexposure. The mottled texture of the natural background of foliage is likewise poor for flight shots. With this setup you merely wait for the insects to fly in or out of the flower across the allotted frame space. The timing of the shutter tripping in coincidence with the chance passage of the insect in the plane of focus determines the degree of success.

Another place to catch insects in flight is at the opening of their nest holes. The caterpillar hunter wasp (*Sphex*), for example, has a regular flight pattern in and out of its hole while it disposes of excavated dirt. Frequently beeflies (*Bombyliidae*) hover over wasp or bee nest holes while they drop eggs in them. Their relatively stationary hovering flight increases the chances of candid flight pictures. In these near-to-the-ground shots, the ground itself can serve as a background. If there are numerous twigs, pebbles, etc., on the ground behind the nest, the photographic background may be simplified by removing these at the outset of the work.

Certain flies, such as syrphid or flower flies, will hover for long periods in one place, and you can, after repeated tries, get pictures of them in flight. If nearby foliage can be aligned as a background, the chances of success will be much better than when you depend on the sky for a background.

OBJECTIVES AND STANDARDS

Now that we have discussed the tools and methods of using them to photograph insects—the most diverse of the earth's creatures—I would like to conclude with a few words of advice.

First of all, you should realize that the mere possession of the proper equipment and a desire to photograph insects does not guarantee success in this endeavor any more than a typewriter, paper, and an urge to write assure success in writing. Photography is one of the arts and, like any other art, it requires considerable effort. If such efforts cannot become a pleasure, you should try something else.

Then there are certain physical requirements, the lack of which no amount of effort or artistry can completely overcome. These requirements are good eyesight, steady hands, coordination, and agility which enables you to stoop, bend, creep, and crawl at insect level, and to do so quickly.

Another qualification for real achievement is some knowledge of insects. Photography is a means of recording visual experience and communicating it from one individual to another. Some visual experiences are trite and scarcely worth recording or communicating. A knowledge of the subject tells the photographer when he has something worth "saying" and when he has succeeded in saying it well. Knowledge thus sets standards of achievement. All too often we see shown or published insect pictures of low quality which indicate that the photographer was easily pleased with mediocre results.

I do not wish to imply that you must be a trained entomologist to contribute in the field of insect photography. Some of the best entomological work has been done by self-taught persons, and most of the best professional entomologists are amateurs at heart who ceaselessly add to the knowledge they gained in their college courses.

One soon learns that much of the art of nature photography is knowing when *not* to take a picture. As in the photography of scenery or people, not every available subject will make a worthy picture. Some insects have little or no photogenic qualities and pictures of them may be only of technical interest. Others encountered may be in poor positions, facing or angled the wrong way; the natural background may be too confused, or too far back to be exposed by the flash; or the individual specimen may be damaged, tattered, or abnormal in other ways. At times position difficulties may be corrected by deliberately frightening the insect in the hope that it will run, jump, or alight in a more favorable posture.

You cannot expect every picture to be a gem suitable for exhibition or publication. Insect pictures so shown usually represent the cream of hundreds of attempts, most of which, though sharply focused and correctly exposed, are lacking in punch.

The ideal picture of an insect—or of anything else, for that matter—tells a story with little or no need of a caption. This means that a clearly identifiable center of interest not only has been well lighted and sharply focused but also portrays some self-explanatory normal, interesting phenomenon. Thus a dung beetle should be seen making, rolling, or burying its ball of dung; a robber fly should be clutching its prey; a butterfly portrait should show a tongue uncoiled and plunged into the depths of a corolla; the mosquito should be biting, laying eggs, or emerging from its pupal case.

Above all, never stage an unnatural encounter or conflict between species. A common form of this is to photograph two "big name" creatures, such as a tarantula and a scorpion, staged in mortal combat. It is difficult for the honest nature photographer to compete with such fakery for publication space in the popular press.

Although storytelling pictures are what we are after, we must often settle for the best picture we can get rather than have none at all. The unceasing appeal of all nature photography is the ever-present potential of upgrading the quality of our own past efforts as well as those of others. Much depends on the element of luck, but the luck of the photographer may be defined as being on the spot at the right time with equipment poised for action. This must be combined with an ability to *see* a picture when it suddenly appears. Being in a position to be "lucky" requires steady, patient effort—seemingly endless wandering and waiting—an effort which can take the devotee to beautiful surroundings and satisfy his hunting instinct in a constructive way.

MARINE LIFE

by Herman W. Kitchen

MARINE photography, now becoming so popular, is by no means a recent development. The last few years have seen the appearance of many new pieces of photographic and diving equipment, and they have spurred interest in the seashore and sea bottom. Even so, marine photography goes way back, almost to the birth of the camera itself.

The first marine photographs probably were taken by Dr. Louis Bouton in 1893. Bouton was a French biologist whose primary interest was natural history. He found the comparatively new invention of the camera convenient to record his observations. The seas and rivers undoubtedly attracted other early photographers as well. Today men are devoting lifetimes to studying and recording, photographically, the life cycles and environments of many marine creatures. The compilation and correlation of all this information add to our store of knowledge. The researchers of the future will have an invaluable store of photographic records upon which to base further research into questions that have perplexed and challenged men from the earliest times. We are looking more and more to the seas and rivers and lakes and ponds for new ways to increase production of foodstuffs. We are also turning to these sources more and more for recreation.

Fishing, swimming, shallow-water diving, and even beach-combing demand that a camera be added to the paraphernalia carried on such jaunts.

This chapter is intended to outline techniques and methods of marine photography and not of photography itself. It is assumed that the reader will have a knowledge of basic photographic principles or can learn these from books devoted especially to the subject. The interested reader should understand how reflected light is transmitted by different lenses, affects different films, and is itself affected by different filters. These are tools which the photographer uses to carve, from the varying volumes of reflected light, pictures in black and white and color, pictures of a hundred varied moods and feelings and a thousand different stories.

KNOWLEDGE OF MARINE LIFE HELPFUL

With a knowledge of photography you will also want some knowledge of your subject. A shell is only a shell until you learn that it is, say, a scallop shell; that a scallop is a bivalve possessing as many as thirty to forty eyes, that by sudden opening and closing of its two shells it can propel itself away from danger. Again, what may look like a beautiful underwater flower to the untutored eye you will know as a sea anemone; what look like petals at its top are the animal's tentacles spread out in wait for unwary bits of life upon which it feeds. Knowing something about the likely subjects you will see will allow you to handle and interpret them more accurately. You are able to watch for those things which show a particular characteristic or tell a story about your subject. You know what to look for and where to find it. You enjoy much more the time spent around water with your camera.

Often you will want to take a series of photographs to create a more revealing story. A single picture of a starfish does not tell anyone as much about this active echinoderm as a series showing the arms or tentacles in different positions during locomotion. A single picture of the hard dorsal surface will not disclose the hundreds of tiny cilia on the ventral surface which cause currents of food-laden water to flow into the mouth of the animal. A single picture of a subject will give you a two-dimensional or—depending on the camera angle and light—perhaps a three-dimensional feeling. Several more pictures of a subject, in various stages of development, will add a fourth dimension to the treatment of that subject. It is this last dimension that rounds out understanding of a subject and adds to the edifice of knowledge.

WARNING TO BEGINNERS

On a camera trip to the seashore, pond, or lake you may go alone, but having a companion along enables you to share the enjoyment of discovery and photography. Moreover, in case of some unexpected situation you and your camera have another pair of hands to rely on for help.

Be careful when walking over rocks that are wet and covered with algae growths. These growths of mosslike plants are very slick and can cause a bad fall. Keep in mind when around tidal areas that it may be easy enough to pick your way over the mud flats or between tide pools at dead low tide, but the incoming tide can make walking hazardous. Never go too far out over tidal flats while the tide is at ebb. The tide may rise faster than you can return to safe land, especially over bottom you cannot see. Camera, film, lenses, and other equipment require some consideration also. Moisture of any kind and particularly salt air can ruin a whole day's trip if you do not properly protect your equipment. The hot sun also can damage a camera, film, or light meter. Keep the gear covered and protected from sun, moisture, and sand when not in use.

A GREAT VARIETY OF SUBJECTS

The marine life that you photograph will depend on where you live and how far you can travel. There may be a backwater bay nearby that offers excellent opportunities. You can spend hours and days getting a series of pictures on the plant life of such a semi-saltwater area. In nearly every region of the country the photographer can easily find a fresh-water pond; from the water-lilies and cattails which everyone knows down to the minute floating duckweed and even microscopic algae or pond scums, there is a world of fascination.

Many insects spend a great part of their lives in an underwater larval stage. Thus they furnish food, year round, for birds, mammals, and amphibians which also visit these semi-marine environments. Photo stories of any of these creatures will include pictures taken during each season, so there are year-round opportunities for marine photography even in one small area.

At the ocean, the subjects may be porpoises or even the largest of animals, whales. A boat can take you within easy camera distance of such creatures spotted from the shore. The plants range from the floating sargassum, or gulfweed, to the giant brown algaes called kelps.

You can travel from clear northern streams and bays to southern swamps and bayous, and from the rocky tidepools of Maine to the coral reefs of the Carribean, and never exhaust the opportunities to interpret and record marine life through your own eyes and your camera lenses. The geater the variety of subjects you photograph, the greater will be the enjoyment and value of your marine photograph collection.

EQUIPMENT

The prospective marine photographer confronts first the question of what equipment to purchase. You will have to decide on a camera, tripod, film, filters, and a light meter. The choice depends not only on cost, weight, and availability but on what type of pictures you are after. You may be interested only in marine scenics or solely in fish. You may want to record general marine ecology. The scope of marine subject matter is so extensive that you can never hope to cover it all; furthermore, the amount of equipment required would defeat any such plans.

Cameras

There are four basic types of cameras from which the photographer can choose. They are the single-lens reflex (Fig. 1), the twin-lens reflex (Fig. 2), the press-type camera (Fig. 3), and the view camera (Fig. 4). The single-lens reflex comes in 35 mm, 2¼ x 2¼, and 4 x 5; the twin-lens reflex in 2¼ x 2¼; the press camera in 2¼ x 3¼, 4 x 5, and 5 x 7. The view camera starts with 4 x 5 film size and goes to 5 x 7 and 8 x 10.

All but the twin-lens reflex and some makes of single-lens reflex cameras have interchangeable lenses. The versatility of cameras with this interchangeable feature is something to consider when buying. Sometimes, when a subject is difficult to approach because of wariness or inaccessibility, a longer-focal-length lens can give close-ups from farther back. With a long lens you often can capture from a distance natural behavior that would not be demonstrated if you had to get closer. So it is advantageous to have a camera that will allow you to use lenses of several different focal lengths. A 35 mm camera that does not have the reflex or through-the-lens viewing and focusing is not as desirable because the photographer will sometimes want to get close-ups of small subjects that necessitate a very close focus, or even extension tubes. Here the ability to view and focus through the lens is most important. The film size is another major consideration.

If you want to have slides for projection, then your best choice would be a 35 mm single-lens reflex. You can, of course, get good black-and-white prints from 35 mm negatives, but these call for slower, fine-grain films and the best of processing and printing. Some engravers will not handle 35 mm for reproduction because of the detailed work necessary to make satisfactory plates. There are several larger-sized single-lens reflex cameras, from 2¼ x 2¼ to 5 x 7. This type avoids the parallax problem because you view through the same lens that

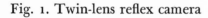

Fig. 1. Twin-lens reflex camera   Fig. 2. Single-lens reflex camera with telephoto lens

takes the picture. You see your subject until the shutter goes off, so you can maintain composition as well as focus even with a moving subject.

The twin-lens reflex camera carries two lenses: one for viewing and focusing, the other for taking the picture. Most makes of this type have no parallax problem down to 36 inches. One popular model can be focused through a set of matching supplementary lenses down to 13 inches without parallax difficulties. This type of camera will give a larger negative and transparency size. Color transparencies from a twin-lens reflex can be cropped down slightly to the new superslides, which give 80 per cent more area than the regular 35 mm size. The superslides are set in the same outside dimension mount, but the inside picture area is larger. Careful processing of the twin-lens reflex black-and-white negative will permit good 8 x 10 enlargements. This 2¼ x 2¼ is the minimum size of color transparencies that most engravers will accept.

The press-type camera goes into a larger film size and is consequently a larger piece of equipment. It is highly versatile, however. The photographer can shoot action pictures or extreme close-ups and also alternate between types of film just by chang-

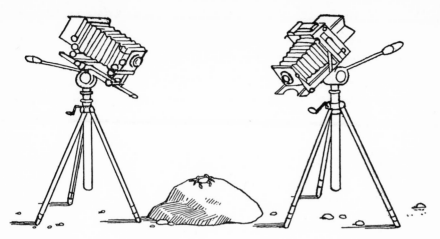

Fig. 3. View camera   Fig. 4. Press-type camera

ing film magazines. The horizontal and vertical swings that the view camera gives either in the lens board or in the film plane are important to consider also. Either end of the camera can be shifted or swung, allowing the photographer to correct any distortion on the ground glass.

The view camera is made in 4 x 5 film size and larger. It is ideal for unhurried situations and studied composing. A tripod is necessary because the focusing is done through the ground glass and then the film magazine is attached. All of these basic camera designs are good; but each one has some advantage over the others for a particular job. Decide what types of pictures you are primarily interested in making, then buy a reputable make.

A photographer can burden himself with many accessories. They all have a purpose and are intended to help in some way, but you can become a slave to gadgets and find less time to get pictures. The more you have to carry, the more complicated becomes the preparation for getting a picture.

Films

The choice of film—color or black and white, fast or slow, fine-grain or not—again depends on the kind of pictures you are after. For 35 mm slides, color is nearly always chosen. If you shoot 35 mm black-and-white film, then a fine-grain, moderately fast film will give better prints. If large salon prints are the object, you will have to use a fine-grain film. Such fine-grain film will permit larger prints without noticeable grain. These films are slower, however, and require either more exposure or slower shutter speeds. If fast shutter speeds are needed to stop action, a fast film is necessary. The color films are all good if you stay within the recommended conditions for using them.

Filters

Filters, if properly used, make possible pictures under conditions that would otherwise defeat your efforts. There are several basic filters that every photographer will frequently need. With either black-and-white or color film a polarizing filter (Pola-Screen) is useful, especially around water. It will decrease the glare from water and other shiny surfaces that are approximately 35 degrees from camera axis. For instance, if you are shooting a subject on the water, without the polarizing filter it would be partly lost. The part that is beneath the surface would be lost because the light is reflecting from the surface instead of from the subject. With color film the polarizing filter can also darken an otherwise white or light blue sky. With black-and-white film, yellow, orange, and red filters give increasingly more contrast, especially if there are sky and clouds in the picture. Filters also cut haze in long marine scenic shots; and for this purpose in shooting color, a so-called haze filter is particularly recommended.

Tripod

A tripod is essential equipment for the marine photographer. He may even need two, one for normal shots and one for those shots at almost ground or water level. There are several tripods, however, that allow the elevator pan head to be taken off and inserted in the tripod from the bottom. Thus the camera can be cranked down to the subject while the legs are spread solidly apart.

Get a sturdy tripod. With slow shutter speeds or long lenses a shaky one can cause the camera to move and blur an otherwise good picture.

Light Meter

A good light meter also can spell the difference between good pictures and bad. Marine photography can take you from shaded streams with low light intensities to open water or sandy beaches where the light is so dazzling that you will have to wear sunglasses. You cannot depend on your eyes to judge lens settings under such varied light conditions. Color films demand even more exact exposures than black and white. With color a good light meter is a necessity and the proper application of one will assure more consistent results.

Lenses

On occasions when you want to move closer to your subject but cannot for some reason, extra lenses are essential. The ideal set of lenses includes a normal-focal-length lens, a wide-angle one of about half the focal length of your normal lens, and a third one about twice the normal focal length.

LIGHTING

The sun will not always be out for your photographic benefit. Artificial light will often be needed. If no electrical sources are available, either flashbulbs or strobe lights will have to be used to illuminate the subject. With either type of light you must follow the film manufacturer's recommendations for exposure. The light illuminating a subject varies inversely with the square of the distance. Thus a distance of only a few feet between light and subject can mean a difference of several stops. When using flash for illumination, keep in mind that you may get reflections that cannot be foreseen. The average subject will not cause any trouble in this respect, but full picture areas of shiny wet surfaces should be carefully studied. Reflections, besides causing hot spots in your pictures, sometimes can also distort color. If either the artificial light source or even sunlight is reflected from a colored surface onto the subject, the true color of that subject can be lost. Be sure that your subject is not being illuminated by light reflected from areas of strong color.

Sometimes you will not use flash for your main light source but only to supplement sunlight. If the sun is very bright and causes the subject to cast a shadow, a flash fill-in light can improve the picture. With an extension cord from flashgun to camera you can control the amount and direction of the fill light. The flash source and film must be balanced for the same color temperature if you are using color film. This would mean blue flashbulbs and daylight film or tungsten film and a proper conversion filter.

Another piece of equipment that will aid lighting efforts is a

Fig. 5

30. Equipped with a SCUBA—Self Contained Underwater Breathing Apparatus —the photographer is free to move about in quest of subjects for his camera.

31. The photographer must watch his step. Creatures such as these sea pests— Sea Urchin and Sting Ray—are interesting and good subjects for the camera, but a brush with either can be very painful.

32. This snapper's retreat is almost hidden by Gorgonians which belong to a group including sea fans, sea pens and sea plumes.

33. A Spiny Lobster. This rather shy crustacean can be enticed from its crevice in the coral by bait. The long antenna sticking out of holes in the coral betray its location.

34. The convolutions of the surface give this Brain Coral its name. Some fish apparently find it an interesting playground.

35. This French Angelfish claims a particular antler coral for its own territory. Such fish are easy to photograph because they do not want to leave their own protective area.

36. Most reef fish such as these Bluestriped Grunts stay close to sheltering corals. Sometimes if they are disturbed they will dash across the open sand to seek refuge under another coral. The feathery growths are sea plumes, another form of coral.

37. This is a garden of animals, not plants. The tall heavy growths are Candle Sponges, the short one like a "chimneypot" in the foreground is the Brown Sponge; the others are corals.

reflector. This can be used to fill in shadow areas and even illuminate subjects out of direct sunlight. For color, of course, use a surface that has no tint or color tone at all. Generally a reflector is made from an aluminum-foil-covered or white-painted surface. Thin plywood or heavy cardboard is often used for the base of a reflector. A leg can be hinged to the back like the brace on the back of a picture frame to prop the reflector at the proper angle. When there is no reflector available, or using one is not practical, you can diffuse sunlight through a white netting or glass cloth stretched over the subject (Fig. 5). This diffused light will give a better picture than direct sunlight, which is often too harsh for good color pictures.

SEASHORE AND TIDE POOL

Many small creatures attach themselves to floating debris in the water and are later cast up on the shore. Along this "sea wrack" you can find small shrimps and crabs that have floated in on seaweeds such as the gulfweed or sargassum weed. These algae are free-floating plants that provide havens of safety for small animals. There also will be old ship timbers or pilings that have washed ashore. Examine these closely for barnacles and the burrows of the teredo, or boring clam. Sometimes timbers will be completely riddled by hundreds of small holes. Tangled in the seaweed you often can find the long necklacelike strands of *Busycon* egg cases. The single egg capsules of skates and some sharks are also to be found here. If you find these small treasures soon after a tide or storm has left them stranded, you will be able to capture the freshness and color that may soon disappear.

Set your tripod and camera up in a convenient spot and carry the subjects to the camera or set your equipment up where you find likely subjects. The first method is probably more desirable where you find several subjects within a small area. You can then spend more time preparing a suitable background, erecting a

diffusion screen, and placing reflectors if necessary. Brush sand
and other debris from the subject, being careful not to break
delicate parts that may have dried brittle. Dip large specimens
in water to add luster or, better still, use a small hand spray to
spray water onto the surface. A thin film of mineral oil rubbed
on a dull subject will add sparkle and bring out delicate colors.
With this semipermanent setup you can photograph more subjects in a shorter period of time.

When the tide is out you will find another area full of life.
This will require some caution however. The bottom, whether
sandy or muddy, will be soft; so watch your step and equipment.
If you are using a tripod put a small can on each tripod leg. The
cans will protect the feet from the salt water and mud and also
give your tripod more support. The period of ebb tide offers
good opportunity to find and photograph clams, mussels, snails,
and some plant life. You will have to dig for clams. Most of
these bivalves live several inches below the surface of the mud
or sand and a shovel is the tool for finding them. Mussels are no
problem to photograph. They are found mostly between the
tides, attached to rocks or pilings. They are sometimes found in
large beds covering several square yards, so there is an opportunity for a good series of pictures. There are several species of
snails that are found between the tides. The periwinkles and
purple sea snails crowd the crevices of rocks, feeding on the
algae and waiting for the next tide. They find enough moisture
in the exposed plant life to sustain life till the incoming tide
reaches them. Under these plants you will find many other small
crustaceans. Limpets and chitons adhere to rocks that are exposed between the tides and are sometimes covered with the
same mosslike algae growth as the rocks around them.

Check the tide pools for starfish, anemones, sea urchins, and
small sponges. The water in a small hole in the rocks will be
calm and often full of life. Take up a position where the glare
on the water will be lessened or use a polarizing filter for the

same effect. Here you will need long extension bellows or tubes, long-focal-length lens, or supplementary lenses to enable you to get close enough to your subjects for a good picture. If you are working on rocks have a tripod that has sharpened points on the legs. These will keep a firmer hold on the slick surfaces. At times you may want to collect several scattered bits of marine life and put them into one small pool to photograph. You could collect several snails, hermit crabs, starfish, and some sea urchins for a composite photograph of tide-pool life. Be certain though that you do not add something that would not ordinarily be found in a tidepool. In any case, such pictures should be labeled "arranged for photography."

Many of the marine creatures, of course, cannot be photographed in their natural habitat: for instance, mollusks that live under the mud and sand. They will have to be removed from the mud and washed so that they can be seen; but you should so indicate when a picture has been taken of a subject out of its normal environment. Many people would be misled by seeing a picture of a spider crab on the sandy beach or in a tidepool with sea anemones. You must make sure that while shooting a photographic story of something you do not unwittingly present an incorrect bit of information. Keep a log of the location, time, and date of your pictures.

SHALLOW WATER

When introduced to new surroundings many marine animals will not display ordinary behavior. So the photographer must go into the shallow water for these pictures. This means that the camera or lens must be under the surface of the water. This can be done in several ways. A glass port can be set into the bottom of a boat, allowing you to see the bottom clearly. Erect a canopy or have a parasol held over your head and the glass port to eliminate glare of the sun and open sky. Bright light falling on the glass port will reflect into the camera lens and your

Fig. 6

eyes. The disadvantage of this method is that the boat will rock and the camera placement will not be as steady as it should be. The best method, in water even chest deep, is some version of the look-box. It can be as simple as a bucket that has the bottom replaced with a piece of glass. Hold the camera inside the bucket and shoot through this clear window in the sea. A simple box can be built that will serve the purpose even better (Fig. 6). A piece of clear, uncolored optical flat glass (to prevent distorting color) is cemented in one end of a square wooden box. On one inside board fasten vertically two grooved strips of wood about four inches apart. These form a channel where a block to which the camera is fastened will slide. A bolt can go through the top edge to hold in the camera block. Next, from a rubberized material cut out a hood somewhat like an old Graflex hood and fasten it securely around the top edge of your camera look-box. You can stiffen this with a wire frame or sew on a loop which will go around your head to keep the hood open. This hood does two things: it keeps water from splashing in on the camera, and it shades the inside of the glass bottom. Use a long cable release so your hands can be supporting the box and still release the shutter. If you use an open box with no hood, have some way to shade the inside so that you will not be troubled with reflections getting into your lens. A companion might hold a parasol over your head. Sometimes a large straw hat will do the same thing.

The size and shape of the box suitable for your needs will depend on the camera. The box should be waterproof. You will want to be able to focus and set the lens easily and you will want to get your eye to the viewfinder quickly and easily.

Another basic design especially for reflex cameras is an oblong wooden box in which a twin-lens reflex can be mounted (Fig. 7). The end that goes into the water is closed and a window is cut into one side near the bottom. The camera is then mounted

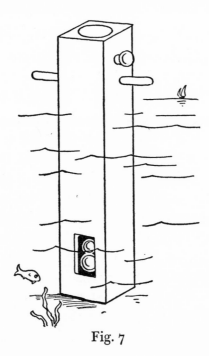

Fig. 7

on a square piece of iron or lead and lowered to the bottom of the box by the camera strap. The weight should be just heavy enough to sink the box about two thirds of its length. The cover for the top will have a simple lens mounted in it to allow you to see that your subject is properly framed and in focus. This lens must have a focal length equal to the distance from cover to reflex finder. You can connect the focusing knob of the camera by an elastic cord to a control knob at the top of the camera box to avoid taking the camera out for each adjustment of focus; otherwise, the lens can be set for a certain distance and the box moved closer or farther from your subject until the image is sharp in the reflex finder.

The best type of sea bottom with which to start your photography is a light, sandy one. Here your subjects will stand out more clearly and the sand will reflect light into otherwise shadowy areas. Of course, a flounder or ray will sometimes change colors to match its surroundings. Usually, just before swimming away these fishes change colors again, and if you are properly prepared you can get your picture then. Many fish come into shallow water to make nests in the sandy or light gravelly bottoms. You can easily spot these saucer-shaped depressions because they are neatly rounded and clean. The female keeps sediment and debris cleaned out by fanning the nest with her tail. If the nest is in use you can usually get quite close to the female, who is guarding her eggs from other hungry fishes. She may swim away for a few minutes, but if you remain still she will return to camera range.

Except for habitat shots, try to photograph your subjects against as plain a background as possible. Many marine creatures, unless they are moving, blend into the background and are hard to see. This is particularly true when they are photographed in black and white. Separate the subject from its background by photographing it against a contrasting color or with the background out of focus. This may sound like a big order, arranging fish underwater, but it can be done.

You can entice fish or eels or crabs out from hiding and into camera range with food. When you have located some likely subjects, have a companion lure them into camera range and against a suitable background with a piece of bait tied to a fishing line. Have the bait suspended to one side of the camera's field of view and photograph the subject as it swims by. Another method, which you can handle by yourself, is to crush a crab, sponge, or sea urchin near a suitable background. Small fish and then larger ones will soon be attracted to the feast. Sometimes there will be so many around that you will have to frighten some away.

When you take your camera underwater there are three more factors to consider. These should be understood in principle from the beginning.

You have no doubt noticed how much larger an object looks underwater than it actually is. The fish that gets away really looks larger because the water magnifies its size. Anytime that light passes through two mediums of different densities, it is bent or refracted. This refraction causes our eyes to receive an image larger than actual size. Besides appearing larger, the object appears closer as well. It will seem a fourth closer and a fourth larger. Thus, underwater photographers who set their lenses at the measured distance may find out later that the pictures are out of focus. Here the advantage of a reflex camera is apparent; you can see that your subject is in sharp focus before shooting.

With a nonreflex camera a special measuring stick is handy. This is a four- or five-foot hollow metal tube about one quarter inch in diameter. Before closing the ends, add enough weight to the inside to give it a slight negative buoyancy. A hardwood dowel can also be used if it is weighted and then varnished. Paint a ring around the rod every 16 inches to represent underwater feet. Do not use red paint. Red light rays decrease with increased depths, so that at some depths and under some light conditions you may not be able to see your marks. Black would be preferable. The camera must be focused at three quarters of the camera-to-subject distance. Thus a subject four feet away would measure three rings on your measuring rod. You would then set the lens focus at three feet. If you do not have a measuring rod, set the lens focus at the apparent distance. The camera lens sees a subject magnified, and apparently closer, the way your eye does.

Another factor to consider is the absorptive quality of water. If the water is clear and the bottom is light-colored sand, exposure readings may be as high as they are above water; but if there is any sediment in the water, the readings will be very low. This cloudy character can be caused by many things. Shallow water is easily stirred up with a surf or running tide, and of course, if you wade through a muddy bottom, it is going to become murky. At certain times of the year millions of microscopic eggs and diatoms are released into the water; they also affect visibility. It is best to take meter readings from about camera position so that your reading will be through the same distance of water that your lens will be shooting. This can be done with a special underwater light meter, but any good meter can be put into a tight-fitting clear-glass jar and provide satisfactory readings.

If you are shooting color film, the color of the water must be taken into account. Different microscopic substances in the water will give it different colors, and you may have to correct off-color water with a filter. Use a color-compensating filter that absorbs the predominant color of the water.

These color-compensating filters are available in several densities and colors. Thus, you have some control over the amount of correction. For instance, if the water is light green, use a CC10M filter; or if the water is a dark green, use up to a CC40M or CC50M. A filter absorbs its complimentary color and transmits its own color. In this case the magenta filter, which is red and blue, absorbs some of the complementary, green, and transmits the red and blue light rays. If you have chosen a filter of the correct color and density combination, and allowed for the necessary exposure increase, you should have a good color photograph. Other CC filters absorb blue, blue-green, yellow, etc. The marine photographer will be mostly concerned with the CC yellow, CC red, and CC magenta series.

AQUARIA

Marine photography includes not only fish, mollusks, and crustaceans of large size but many minute, fragile creatures as well. Some can be photographed from the seaside or shores and others by divers. There are, however, many marine creatures that cannot be photographed in their natural environment well or at all. Wildlife should be photographed in its natural habitat, but sometimes this is not possible. Then the photographer must resort to an aquarium in order to arrange and light a subject for good record or illustration photographs—particularly when shooting in color. Colors of a picture taken in the normal habitat may not be accurate because of varying depths in which the subject is found; also, the water may be discolored by different kinds of sediment. Small transparent shrimps and jellyfish polyps and tiny delicate hydroids are difficult to photograph in the open water. The photographer can either set up a salt-water aquarium and camera on the shore or carry the collected animals home to photograph.

If you want to set up an aquarium near your collecting location find a smooth, light-colored sandy spot. The light-colored sand will reflect some light into the aquarium so that you get good diffused lighting. Harsh, direct sunlight can be further controlled by erecting over the aquarium a diffusing net of white material. Be sure to wash everything that you put into the aquarium to prevent the water from becoming clouded with fine sediment, which takes a long time to settle to the bottom.

At home, place the aquarium on a table about waist high and a foot or two from the wall. A sheet of glass or clear plastic just large enough to fit inside the aquarium parallel to the front glass is essential to keep your subjects in a narrow field of focus. Because your camera is so close to your subjects, the depth of field is very small and this transparent sheet will keep the subjects near the front of the aquarium.

When collecting fragile shrimps, worms, jellyfish, and others, it is a good idea to dip them up in a fine net. You can then dip the net in the aquarium and turn it inside out to release the animals. You can also use a jar or shallow dish to pick up specimens from the surface. Do not put too many specimens in the aquarium at one time, for the scene will then be too busy for a good illustration photograph.

You may plan to carry sea water and specimens to an indoor aquarium. There you can have a more permanent setup with controlled lighting and separate specimen tanks. Remember that many of the marine animals prefer certain temperatures and light intensities and will not act naturally otherwise. The sea water will have to be changed every day or, better still, continually pumped from the sea itself. Consult a good aquarium guide on how to maintain a marine aquarium if you wish to keep one indefinitely. To transport delicate specimens without damage, fill a container completely full of water, put in your specimens, and cover with a tight lid. If there is no splashing around in a container, there will be no damage. Of course, no aeration is possible in a completely closed container, so the specimens should be transferred to an open tank as quickly as possible.

Whether the photographic equipment that you use is complicated or simple, you can take good pictures. All that is necessary is a camera, light meter, tripod, and some lights. Your camera is mounted on a sturdy tripod which is fastened to a plywood base. This allows the tripod to be moved about and still be safe from falling. Lights can be placed on stands to the front and sides of the aquarium. They should be directed at an angle of about 45 degrees to the surface of the water. This angle for the lights is important for several reasons. First, it simulates the natural angle of the sunlight; and second, you will be directing the light, which is warm, at the water and not at the glass. Sometimes, when a glass plate of an aquarium full of cool water is heated, the difference in temperature on either side of the glass will cause it to crack. If you use lights close to the water, put a piece of wire screen over the top in case a light or something else falls. The lights should be just close enough or intense enough to enable you to use normal shutter speeds and an *f* stop that will give you enough depth of field. Lights should not be set so close that the water will become warm. Use a sheet of glass or plastic as before to confine your particular subject to the front of the aquarium. Behind this and slightly out of focus you can arrange an appropriate background of eelgrass or other marine plants.

If you are using a reflex camera, focusing or composing a picture will be no problem. However, if you are using extension tubes and do not have through-the-lens viewing, you must calculate the focus and field of view carefully. Instructions and focusing charts are generally supplied with extension tubes and supplementary lenses. Follow these guides carefully and use a small *f* stop, which will give you more depth of field and margin of safety. To find the field of view of your lens open the back of the camera before loading it with film and insert a piece of ground glass in the film plane. Then mark the four corners of your field of view on the front glass of the aquarium. Now mark out a rectangle just slightly larger than the four corner marks. This will be your field of view and the proper position for your subject to be in for photographing. For some of the very delicately lined and light-colored jellyfish, comb jellies, and other transparent or translucent animals, you will want to use back lighting. This will make the fine internal structure of the animal stand out sharply. With conventional front lighting the delicate colors are lost.

There are many public aquaria stocked with beautiful and exotic marine life. They are generally well lighted and kept clear so that good photographs can be taken with black-and-white film, and in some of the brighter-lighted ones color pictures can be taken. Most aquaria will not allow floodlights or flashbulbs to be used for picture taking; therefore you will have to use faster films and slower shutter speeds if possible. Filters will be needed where the water is discolored with algae or sediment. A conversion filter may be necessary also, depending on the type of illumination in the tank. If fluorescent lights are used, daylight film will give satisfactory results. Low-wattage mazda lamps burn reddish, or warmer in photographic language, and will require tungsten-type film or a conversion filter with daylight film.

The Marine Studios at Marineland, Florida, have many convenient portholes through which the photographer can take pictures. Another fine aquarium is at Paradise Beach in Nassau, where the tanks are well illuminated and contain a wide assortment of colorful reef fishes and native Bahama corals. Again let me emphasize that all pictures taken of controlled or captive specimens be labeled as such. At Silver Springs, Florida, "Photo Subs" are available for the photographer who wishes to go underwater without getting wet. These are roofed-over boats with deep wells in which to sit and look through underwater portholes. Glass-bottomed boats are available, too, in many other fine underwater areas such as Wakulla Springs, Florida.

UNDERWATER TECHNIQUES

Marine photography of any kind is exciting and rewarding. The experiences of underwater photography, however, are incomparable. You will be entering a completely different world with your first dive. It is an indelible experience to lie suspended in midwater without the tug of gravity on your body and then, with a flick of your flippers and an arching of your body, to cruise through space below the rocking boat and above the forests of kelps, corals, and other sea life of the bottom.

There are several psychological and physiological factors that you will have to become familiar with before going to the bottom with your camera. First of all, there is in some people an almost inherent fear of the sea and its creatures. Familiarity will dispel these fears for those who are observant and want to know the truth. The only thing to fear is yourself. Nearly all uncomfortable incidents are caused by carelessness or lack of sufficient knowledge.

Know your diving gear well and keep it in good condition. Know the water you are diving in and know some of the life that you will encounter. You would not play with hornets or wade through poison ivy; you know better. They do not keep you from walks in the woods either. The same goes for the life that inhabits the oceans and sea floors. Learn what to look out for and be cautious of what is new to you. There is a fine little booklet, *Sea Pests,* available at most diving-equipment dealers, which describes various poisonous and harmful sea life. With a knowledge of these "pests" that you may encounter in underwater jaunts, you will feel more secure and confident in your picture taking. Most of the tales of attacks by sharks and giant octopuses are creations of wild imaginations.

Physiologically, there are some inherent reactions to overcome. Pressure is one. As you descend, the pressure will become noticeable first in your ears then over your whole body. This new sensation is nothing to worry about if you are careful. The pressure on your body is no problem. The only concern will be your ears. The change in pressure that affects your ears when you fly is felt when diving, but in reverse and more so—for water is much denser than air. A dive to 33 feet incurs twice as much of a pressure change as a flight to 18,000 feet. If you dive without a breathing apparatus of some sort, the pressure will build up against your eardrums and cause some discomfort. Dives like this to greater depths can even cause a puncture of the eardrums, so it is not advisable to go deep without breathing gear. Do not use ear plugs that are sold only to keep water out of the ears of swimmers, not divers. If you dive with them the pressure may force them so far into the ear that you cannot get them out.

Photography in Shallow Water

There are several methods of photographing underwater. The first is from the surface into shallow water perhaps only over your head. A face mask, snorkel, and flippers are all the diving equipment necessary. (We will discuss underwater cameras shortly.) The face mask will permit you to see comfortably and will keep your nose covered as well. Through the snorkel you can breathe easily. One end is held in the mouth and the other is projected out of the water like a periscope. Rubber feet or flippers aid in swimming and maneuvering underwater. You swim on the surface face down, looking for a likely subject. When you sight something, take a breath, dive down to it, get your picture, and return to the surface. Many good pictures are taken this way because much of the marine life and the best color will be found in such comparatively shallow water. Some people may find that a weighted belt is necessary to enable them to dive easily. Do not try to inflate your lungs completely before a dive, because it is too tiring. Just take a full breath, let part of it out, then dive.

Diving Gear

There are three types of diving gear that will enable you to make sustained dives. They use either compressed air, inert gases with oxygen, or air and oxygen, depending on the diving requirements and type of equipment. The oldest and probably best known is the diving helmet with an air hose to a surface pump. A continual stream of air is pumped into the helmet, which is worn over the head and shoulders. You must remain upright in this gear; otherwise the air will spill out and the water rush in to cover your head. This kind of diving helmet has the advantage of enabling you to remain on the bottom longer than other types of gear permit. It does require an operator on the surface, so it is not as versatile as the Aqua Lung or SCUBA type, which is becoming so popular these days.

The SCUBA (Self-Contained Underwater Breathing Apparatus) incorporates a pressure-compensating valve to regulate the compressed air from a tank worn on the back of the diver. The pressure delivered fom the tank is equal to the pressure of the water on your body, so that you are able to breathe comfortably at any depth. You must flex your jaws, though, to allow the pressure inside the ear drum to equal that on the outside from the water. As you descend or ascend, you will have to equalize the pressure this way.

The third type of underwater equipment is a rebreather apparatus. With this unit you breath into an enclosed bag of air. The exhaled air is filtered through Beralyme crystals for purification, and an adjustable trickle of oxygen replaces that which you use. No bubbles are released from this unit, so it is preferred by some divers. There is a distinct limit, though, to the depth at which it can be used. Oxygen under pressure greater than one additional atmosphere of 33 feet of depth is poisonous. Most of your photography will probably be done at no greater depths, but this limitation should be kept in mind when you consider the purchase of underwater breathing gear.

A diving suit is a welcome item at times, especially in northern or West Coast waters. Even in the comparatively warm waters around the Gulf Stream, you will lose much body heat after several hours in the water. There are two types of suits, wet

Fig. 8. The underwater photographer completely equipped with SCUBA, diving suit, and waterproof camera case.

and dry. The dry suits are just that—they keep you dry. The wet suits are not sealed and you do become wet, but the close-fitting spongy material keeps the water from circulating over your body and retains much of your body heat.

A weight belt will enable you to establish an equilibrium for swimming. You should have enough weight in it so that when you inhale from your air tank you will rise, and when exhaling will sink. For working on the bottom you will want more weight to make walking easier. Be sure that this belt has a quick-release so it can be removed quickly if necessary. An emergency "Rescue Pack," which is a plastic water wing inflated by a squeeze on the CO_2 cartridge inside, is a good safety measure for yourself and your equipment.

Underwater Cameras

Several types of cameras are used successfully underwater. But they are in the smaller film sizes. 35 mm cameras are popular because of economy and the number of exposures available with one loading. They are comparatively easy to enclose in a waterproof or watertight housing if you wish to construct your own. There are, however, several models of 35 mm cameras available with special underwater cases. They have focusing and aperture controls, film-advance lever, parallax-correcting view-finders, and even underwater flashguns. Twin-lens reflex cameras in the 2¼ x 2¼ film size are popular also. They do not give as many exposures per loading but they have the advantage of enabling you to focus on your subject. Also, they eliminate any problem with parallax at normal subject distances.

Many marine photographers prefer the twin-lens Rolleiflex with its Rolleimarin case for underwater use. You can focus through the reflex viewer, select a filter, and adjust aperture and shutter speed with easy-to-operate controls. Film advance is rapid and reloading is done quickly and conveniently. The lens can be focused down to 36 inches and, with a slight modification, a set of close-up supplementary lenses can be used to allow focusing to 13 inches. Another popular practical camera is the Fenjohn Goggler. This is an "underwater camera"—that is, a watertight camera, not just a camera in a watertight case. It takes standard 120-size film and can take bulk loads of 70 mm film. It is not a reflex camera, however, and the focus must be estimated or the distance measured.

Flashguns are available for both of these cameras. They are easily attached and handle either large or small flashbulbs. Strobe lights are increasingly popular and the convenience of a permanent flashbulb or flashtube is worth considering. However, if the unit is not properly made, the high voltage can be dangerous underwater. A good marine strobe unit, with any number of lightheads, is made by Photo Lectronic Research of New York City, which specializes in special outdoor strobe lights.

Special Problems Underwater

Water has properties that the marine photographer will have to become acquainted with and take into consideration when planning a picture. The first and perhaps most important is the light-absorptive quality. If there is sediment caused by turbidity or blooming of miscroscopic plants, the light reaching the bottom will be lessened, for the small particles absorb part of the light. This affects the exposures and also the color.

For precise exposures a light meter should be used. The Fenjohn Company of Philadelphia makes two models of underwater light meters which can be set by external controls. The meter can also be mounted inside a tight-fitting clear jar. Set the meter for the film speed, then calibrate a small card with the different light readings you would expect to get underwater. Next to each calibration have several possible shutter speed–aperture combinations. For example, a Weston film speed of 24 and a reading of 100 would give you these combinations: 1/25 at f 11, 1/50 at f 8, 1/100 at f 5.6, and so on. This card can be taped to the inside of the meter jar or, if waterproofed, to the camera case.

Remember that a meter averages the light reflected from the whole scene it covers; if your subject is darker than the background, compensate accordingly. This may mean opening the aperture an f stop or more. Conversely, if the subject is lighter than the background, close the aperture.

Your meter cannot compensate for the color of the light reflected from a scene. The color unbalance underwater is caused by two things. First, water absorbs light rays, varying with the different light wave lengths. Red is the first to be affected, then orange, then yellow, and so on down the spectrum to the blues. Reds are completely lost in about thirty feet of clear water. If the water has impurities, the reds will be lost in less depth. The impurities are the second cause for underwater color unbalance. This may stem from such elements as planktonic bloomings, colored minerals in suspension, and yellowish or brownish pigments from underwater plant growth. The marine photographer can only compensate partly for these by use of filters which will absorb the predominant color of the impurities.

In clear water five or six feet deep there is seldom need for filters, but as you go deeper and the red rays are filtered out you will need them. With a reddish filter you will be able to absorb the amount of green and blue light that is predominant over the red and reach a near balance of color. This is only practical to depths of around twenty feet, since approximately 50 per cent of the red is lost at ten feet and all red is lost at thirty feet. Figure on ten additional points of filter density for each additional five feet of depth; thus, at fifteen to twenty feet you would be using a CC-40R.

There are filter factors to consider. For example, up to a CC-20R the factor will require an exposure increase of one third of a stop. The denser CC-30R and CC-40R will require about a full stop more exposure. With black-and-white-film contrast filters you can cut down the haziness of long underwater shots. They are not as effective below water as above because there are less red, orange, and yellow rays to affect your film underwater.

For the problem of magnification of objects underwater, as stated before, the best solution is a reflex camera which you can focus through the lens. If your camera cannot be focused in this way, the judging or measuring of distance must be done carefully. If you measure the distance, set your camera at three quarters of the actual camera-to-subject distance. If you are estimating the distance, set the camera at the apparent distance of the subject. The camera lens is misled by the refraction of water as much as your eye is.

Underwater Photography

The most interesting and photogenic place to begin your photography is around large coral heads, wrecks, or boulders. These features attract many marine creatures because there are holes and crevices for the smaller ones to escape into, and, in turn, this concentration of small fishes and crustaceans attracts larger fish. If the area has not been disturbed by much human activity, you will have little trouble getting good close pictures. Fish, like all creatures, soon learn to avoid man when his actions are harmful.

By slowly swimming around, without any quick movements, you will be able to approach many fish. Sometimes, out of curiosity, fish will swim directly up to your camera lens and even up to your face mask. They seem fascinated by eyes or by the glass plates of the mask and camera case. This curiosity can be used to your advantage if you remain in one spot and allow the fish to swim into camera range. Set the lens at a predetermined distance and wait for the fish to swim into that range. This "still shooting" has another advantage besides being easier on the photographer—it allows pictures to be taken at slower shutter speeds. The camera is held steadier when you are still, and a fish will approach you slower and more smoothly than you could approach it. Sometimes a grouper or barracuda will follow at a distance behind a swimmer, but will not come close enough to be photographed. Have a companion lead such a fish past while you remain still on the bottom. Most fishes will become alarmed only by sudden movements, so raise your camera slowly to get the picture.

To attract fish to your camera you can crush a sea urchin or crab, or turn over a piece of coral or rock where the fish will find worms and crustaceans. Have your camera preset and wait for a good shot.

Keep the background as simple as possible. A fish should contrast in color and/or in size with its background. A small fish might be lost against the detail of a cluttered bottom where a larger one would stand out well. Barracudas, which swim close to the surface, are often lost in a picture because they blend into the blue of the infinite water background. You will have to get above them or lure them against a darker coral head or bottom.

To entice octopuses, moray eels, lobsters, and certain fish from caves or dens, tie a piece of fish to the end of a spear. Hold the fish near the entrance to lure the subject out into good light; or better, have a companion do this while you remain ready to get the picture. Never hold wounded fish or bait in your hands; some of the eels and barracudas are fast and may take more than is being offered.

For some close, contrasty scenes you can use flash to fill in the shadow areas. You can use any standard flashbulb and its aperture-distance index to compute exposures; but place the flash half the camera-subject distance or divide the index in half. This is because the water absorbs light from the source to subject to camera. Use regular clear flashbulbs, which are normally too red for color film, because the water will absorb most of the red light and render subjects beyond three feet in natural color. If the subject is closer than three to four feet, hold the flash so that the light will have to pass through eight or ten feet of water from the source to subject to camera.

Reflectors can also be used to furnish fill light underwater. These can be made from varnished pieces of marine plywood painted on one side with aluminum paint. Reflectors are of value only in brightly lit shallow water. In deeper water the light is more diffused and there is little to be reflected.

When you change film, whether on shore or in a boat, be careful to protect it from direct sunlight. It is easy to fog film on bright beaches and in open boats. If possible, change the film under a canopy or umbrella; better still, have someone else change the film for you because you will probably be wet and your hands will be salty. Cameras are extremely susceptible to corrosion from salt water.

The success of the photographer will depend on his knowledge of fish and other marine life as well as on having the best of diving and photographic equipment. This knowledge will come by careful observation and study of the life he encounters on the bottom.

PLANTS

by Rutherford Platt

OF COURSE I am biased about this as I have spent twenty years pursuing the members of the Plant Kingdom with eight cameras and all sorts of accessories and attachments. But I sincerely believe that photography of plant life with just one camera, and whether you take black and white or color, offers a guarantee of the most exciting variety and the surest rewards, including deep satisfaction such as that felt by a lover of poetry.

The plant photographer is confronted with a scale of opportunities, from the colossal, such as big trees on big mountains, to the microscopic, such as pollen jewelry and the finely etched glass boxes of diatoms. Everywhere between these far limits you encounter categories, for example, *gardens*. I know one man who makes a good living by concentrating on gardens. People get surprises when they see beauty and imagination in the corners of their gardens revealed in this man's photographs, which they had not seen when they looked at the original.

Look at *trees*. I have had great recreation taking trees across America, from the most easterly, a red spruce by the lighthouse on Lubec Point, Maine, to the most westerly, the Monterey cypress tortured photogenically on the cliff above the Pacific Ocean at Monterey Point, California; from the highest, a white-barked pine in the snow on Mount Hood, Oregon, to the most southerly, a gumbo limbo whose limbs undulate horizontally like huge fire hoses at Key West, Florida. Each tree was captured as opportunity afforded and put away—and the file has been drawn on continuously through the years by magazines and textbook and encyclopedia publishers. Such pictures are never out of date. You do not have to travel far to build up a file of tree photographs because trees fall into regional categories. There are trees of the northeastern United States, of the Midwest, the Far West and mountains, the Pacific Coast, the South, and the southwestern deserts. Just on week ends, and within a radius of a couple of hundred miles, you can find enough trees to keep you busy and excited, though you take nothing else.

The wildflowers of any locality make another great category. I shall have more to say about this presently. And consider other less obvious opportunities that plants present to the photographer: grasses, ferns, mosses, mushrooms, lichens, seaweeds, leaves with their eccentric contours and the amazing radial symmetry of their vein patterns, the architecture of buds and the dynamics of their opening, seed pods, fruits and berries, details of bark, and parts of flowers such as stamens, pistils and nectar guides, cut-flower arrangements and dry arrangements. If you concentrate on any one of these categories you will find so much for your camera lens that you will feel both exhilaration and frustration because you cannot record it all in one lifetime.

The *prettiest* picture I ever took was an elm tree in the freshness of June with a farmhouse, a pond, and a cow. It was a pleasure to take, but conventional, and I felt no unusual sense of exaltation. The scene was glimpsed by chance while driving along the road, and I was not consciously aware that the angle of the sun was just right and that "this is it!" Later I put the picture away as one of many casual shots. A year or so later *Life* magazine wanted a photograph to symbolize peace and contentment, and in looking through my files this elm tree was encountered. The editors saw a simplicity and eloquence that I had missed and almost lost in the abundance of my tree pictures —and this chance shot was spread across two pages of the magazine.

The moral of this fable is that I had taken the time to stop, get out of the car, and shoot. It was good luck that taught me a lesson. Many's the "great shot" never taken because you are tired, or somebody has to get somewhere, and cars are fast, and traffic is a demon that sweeps you on.

The *most surprising* picture I ever took was after plodding across winter fields and it was cold and the sun was about to set and I thought I had finished a day of photographing tree bark illuminated by clear sunlight and reflections from the snow. There was another frame in the roll and to finish it I shot tree trunks straight toward the sun. What happened was that I had inadvertently captured an instant and an angle when a great light burst through the woodland and the quiet giants of life stood serenely in the light with a quality of awe and depth, and the vision became marvelously dynamic with diverging shadows of the tree trunks rushing at you across the snow. Here was a picture taken only to finish a roll of film, when the light of day was all but gone and this photographer was tired and cold, and making for home. The picture was not only published by *Life* but also used as a frontispiece in one of my books. It also taught another lesson. It opened my eyes, gave me a viewpoint. Ever since then I have been interested in the dramatic possibilities of shooting directly into a low sun.

The *luckiest* pictures I have ever taken were on a dismal, hopelessly drizzly, foggy day. I had gone out to take tree silhouettes in the late fall. It was impossible to scan the landscape for good subjects as you could see hardly a couple of hundred feet. Also, you do not take a valuable camera out of the car in a drizzle. I was discouraged by the weather, but, caught a hundred miles off base, decided to shoot from inside the car at trees that marched out of the fog. My feeling was that it was a waste of film but there was nothing else to do. That was a long time ago—and those were the first photographs I ever had accepted for publication. I learned that the bare branches of a tree have such rhythm and symmetry that they make a complete and beautiful composition without any other element added. The fog blotted out distracting surroundings, and the branches and twigs were sharply etched on a silvery gray background. I also learned that when you have taken something different, perhaps because of adverse conditions, you may get a special story out of it when you look at it after it is printed. In this case the pictures were published with an article on two full pages of the *Christian Science Monitor,* under the title of "Trees in Winter—Far from losing their beauty with their leaves, many reveal new personalities in their trunks and branches."

The *most exciting* picture I ever took was in the early fall when red cedars and shrubs are draped with the fascinating cantilever bridges of the garden spider. All set with close-up attachment for the master builder in the center of its wheel, suddenly a grasshopper leaped into the trap, about four inches from the spider. The Contax turned to a new frame in a second, and by working fast I could get the whole sequence, from the waiting to the winding and stinging, and back to the waiting, this time in great anticipation. This was just luck and there is no moral except that the plant photographer, if he does not look out (or I should say, if he *does* look out), will find himself encroaching on the territory of the insect photographer. My defense is that a spider is not an insect.

Akin to this exciting picture, and with more emphasis on plant photography, was the time I was set up with close-up attachment and focused on a gorgeous fringed gentian. At that moment a bee dropped onto the gentian, fought its way through the folded fringe, and plunged in with only its big behind sticking out. I got a beautiful close-up shot of this dramatic act of pollination that is so swift, so hit-or-miss, it usually is beyond the reach of a still camera. The moral of this fable is that if you keep at it long enough the law of averages is on your side to bring good luck and occasional exceptional pictures which will bring you the perhaps undeserved reputation that helps to sell other pictures of yours which are more run-of-the-mine.

My *most troublesome* photograph was taken in northern

Greenland of a single poppy plant with a dozen blooms all by itself in front of a boulder painted with lichens. The problem was to climb a slope of loose stones so steep that footholds had to be gouged out and camera, tripod, and case of accessories had to be carried in relays between boulders that offered resting spots. In setting up, every move had to be made slowly and thought through in advance. After the picture was exposed, using a mirror to see the adjustments on the front of the camera, the return trip became almost impossible because of slipping stones. The object was to get the camera with the picture inside and the person of the photographer down without taking the shortest and quickest route which was so obvious for a thousand feet. At this point the photographer regrets that he ever got involved in this ridiculous business of taking pictures of the Plant Kingdom. He stops the slipping by lying flat and stretching out his arms and legs to make as much contact with the stones as possible, while all his equipment is strapped to him and almost strangling him. Then he moves his foot a few inches and digs out a little hole with his toes. He moves, inch by inch, and flat on his stomach, dragging the world's most valuable camera equipment by his neck. He brings back the photograph! The moral is to bring back the photographer with the picture.

My *most extraordinary* photograph caught six hot-air balloons bubbling out of the tip of a milkweed pod. We have all seen the dangling balls of milkweed flowers, followed by the big up-turned pods. Famous are the parachute seeds that come out of those pods and sprinkle the hedgerows with their cotton which some people consider mussy, spoiling the neatness of nature. These parachute seeds do not just tumble out of their pods. Their emergence is one of the most interesting routines in nature, seldom observed because it happens so gently and quickly. The milkweed pod is triggered by warm dry sunlight. On such a day in August the air stirs gently. It is the perfect day to be on the beach where most photographers are taking pictures of girls in bathing suits. A little way inland the heat of the sunlight is causing the milkweed pods to split and the two sides to curl back, beginning at the tip. Underneath, brown flat seeds are tightly laid together in spiraling rows like segments of a pine cone. Under the seeds is a glistening mass of wet "cotton." When the sun penetrates this cotton it dries fast, but instead of fluffing out, as you might suppose, it swells up. The strands are caught together both where they are attached to a seed and at their tip ends which are still attached to the core. They are acting like hot-air balloons! The air caught inside is warmed by the sun as it pours through the reflecting silk. In a few moments the balloon is ready to ascend. It leaves the core and rises vertically into the gently stirring air. This is an amazingly deft method for seed scattering, which avoids the seeds falling in a heap around the base of the parent plant. Of course, a few moments after they have risen, the moist silk is dried still more, the tips separate, and the parachute is spread for a gradual descent that will carry the seed a little farther, depending on the breeze.

It is almost impossible to get these quivering little milkweed hot-air balloons in focus outdoors, especially to photograph them swelling one after the other. I used a method, which I consider legitimate, for complete control in front of my close-up attachment. This was to clamp a fresh pod to hold it steady and then substitute for sunlight a spotlight from a Spencer microscope lamp that has a condenser to concentrate the beam and make it warmer and brighter. The spotlight acted like sunlight on the mechanism of the pod. It opened obediently at the tip; the hot-air balloons swelled in succession. I caught beautiful pictures revealing just how this event takes place much better than words can describe it. Experimenting pays off.

SEASONAL DIVERSITY

You can see by what has just been said that the photography of plants is unrestricted. Opportunities of entirely different kinds follow each other through all the seasons of the year. Also, you can take plant pictures at any time that the spirit moves, rain or shine, outdoors or indoors.

However, the very abundance of the subjects calls for caution and discipline. Otherwise there is so much diversion that you do not concentrate long enough on any subject to make a careful study of it—which is the basis of good photography.

You play it by the weather, by the season, and by the camera setup. There are certain days when conditions are fine for landscapes, trees, mountains, and lakes with striking cloud effects. A clear day in winter with snow on the ground is great for tree bark. Sunlight pours over the trunk without interference from leaves, and reflection from the snow illuminates the shadows. You would not imagine that bark is so beautifully sculptured until you see it under those conditions.

That is the general approach, but the photographer must be on the alert in his mind's eye to see charming exceptions. For example, if you are taking smooth silvery bark such as that of beech for pictorial affect more than for identification, your picture will be more interesting with the play of leaf shadows on the bark. And white birch trunks make a prettier picture in summertime against dark blue water.

Certain plants are more colorful and vivid in winter. I am thinking of lichens, mosses, and some ferns—not to mention winter buds. Individual lichens and mosses need close-up treatment, which I shall come to later. But the first approach to all plants is in the way you see them outdoors. Lichens form fanciful patterns on tree trunks, fences, and stones. When you are out for lichens you must look for them and nothing else. They emerge in winter light, coming out of the shadows with beautiful tints and eccentric and exciting outlines suggesting maps and landscapes taken from high in the air. Akin to the lichens are the wonderful woody brackets of the fungi, which emerge from the shadows at the same time. When you are looking for lichen maps on tree trunks in the winter sunlight, you are likely to see a shelf bracket of polished mahogany red. More common are the multicolored brackets with concentric rings on white birchbark. Both the lichens and the brackets are found in greatest abundance on dead stumps and fallen trees in the woods.

You will find interesting lichen pictures in winter on old tombstones. A graveyard in Nova Scotia, used for 250 years and still in use, offered me amazing lichen subjects. This is the only way I know to find the approximate age of lichens. These plants are very slow growing, and there is nothing in their size or features to tell their age. But when you see entirely different kinds of lichens growing on different tombstones, where the engraved time chart covers 250 years, you have a good idea of how long it takes for the different lichens to grow.

Mosses appear brighter green and pink and more lush in winter than any other time of the year. Probably this is an optical illusion because of the brighter light on them. Of course you cannot find much moss if there is deep snow. The ideal condition for moss photography is just after the snow melts away from the edges of brooks and ponds and the bases of trees. Then the moss is beautiful, contrasting bright green, brightened by illumination from nearby snow patches.

Concentration is of first importance in photographing plants. There is a time of year and a day for each category. When you are going after garden pictures you are not concerned with bark or buds. Or if you are after trees you are not thinking about flowers. You may want to build a file on orchids, and another time on dahlias, and during certain weeks in spring you concentrate on buds opening. So on ad infinitum.

Wildflowers are the most alluring and the most frustrating of all subjects for the plant photographer. They have entirely different problems at different seasons. They fall into four groups.

Early Spring

These are the most exciting and the most famous, and yet the hardest to photograph because they are the smallest, weakest, and quickest to fade. They are typically woodland plants that bloom on the floor of the woods when the sun warms and brightens the ground before the leaves come out. These are Jack-in-the-pulpit, violet, spring beauty, bloodroot, trout lily, hepatica. I do not forget that crocus, snowdrop, and grape hyacinth bloom in the early spring on the lawn.

It is a top-notch adventure to become involved in photographing early spring flowers. You have to work fast, as the time between the melting of the snow, thawing of the ground, and the expansion of the leaves is brief. When leaves are on the trees they blot out early spring flowers with shadows. I think of this time of special opportunity as lasting about two weeks, although you can lengthen it by following the spring north, as Edwin Way Teale does, or following it higher up the mountains.

Certain early spring flowers are larger and easier to photograph than those I have mentioned. I am thinking of skunk cabbage and marsh marigold from bogs and beside streams. There is no flower more rewarding, whether in black and white or color, than skunk cabbage. No abstract sculpturing has more arresting pictorial values. The bulbous hood rises to a peak and then curves and twists. Within there is a small lemon-shaped object stuck full of yellow "cloves," and the whole fanciful thing is mottled with purple stripes. Skunk cabbage is tough enough to take out of the bog so that you can study it with flash or floodlight. But wear tall hunting boots or galoshes when you go after it, as the bog pulls off rubbers. This is the early spring flower for the most pictorial fun.

Late Spring

These are less of a challenge to the photographer; they are easier to find and to take. Late spring flowers include the conspicuous flowering shrubs and small trees. Dogwood is the outstanding subject for the camera. Its flower is big and white, with a definite geometric pattern. Moreover, the tree spreads its flowers in artistic horizontal planes. Try to find a way to point down on these spreading flowers to do them justice, or you will get the petals too much edgewise to show up well. The neat dogwood tree is small enough to fit your frame so that it is easier to isolate than most trees, but also close-up clusters of the flowers make marvelous photographs. The fruit trees are also in bloom at this time—apple, cherry, peach. From Pennsylvania westward and southward the redbud tree commands attention for its purple flowers. However, this tree traps many photographers into wasting their film. The purple-red flowers look like nothing in black and white, unless you are expert with filters to bring them out. Even in color they fool you, for they need overexposure to bring into the photograph the conspicuous colors the eye sees. Forsythia first, and later lilac, are among the famous shrubs waiting to have their pictures taken in late spring.

Look in the open woods where there are patches of sunlight, or along the edges of woods. You will find a wealth of wildflowers that make late spring the time most people are thinking of when they speak of spring wildflowers. Here are Dutchman's breeches, rue anemone, wild columbine, and geraniums. Ben Hur Lampman, America's great writer of whimsey and nature essays, must have known the feelings of a photographer ardently after wildflower pictures when he said:

> But if you prefer to look for scarlet columbine,
> Why go look for scarlet columbine.
> There is no other urgency that will not wait.

In Virginia and westward the fire pink must be found at this time to get a memory and a picture thrilling the year round. The same is true of azaleas on stony hillsides. But also, northern states, such as Connecticut, which has the wild azalea for its state flower, produce fine azalea displays. On the floor of the woods, partridge berry, bunchberry, and Canada mayflower are in their prime. Early buttercups and mustards turn fields to dazzling yellow. I have taken several color shots of these bright-yellow spring fields, with a deep blue sky and a red barn to take the breath away. However, when pointing to them with pride later, I was told that those gorgeous displays of mustard are an insult to the farmer, for they betoken neglect of his fields. The photographer should not show his mustard picture to the owner of the property.

Early Summer

These flowers get a running start in late spring. They are a culmination of the flowers that need the long day of sunlight for blooming. This is the time to go after wild roses, especially in the northern states and along the seashore. Wild roses are rife in Maine. The light is great and the flower photographer has no alibi. He might as well go fishing if he cannot get superb pictures of wild roses. I am inclined to think the same way about daisies, black-eyed Susans, evening primrose, and milkweed. They are all big enough for every lens, they come in early summer when the weather is good, and there are plenty to choose.

Late Summer and Fall

Wildflower photography does not consider merely a flower or a group of flowers as constituting the best wildflower picture, unless you are making close-up portraits of individual flowers for identification. Plants are outdoor subjects and the setting helps to tell the story. Roadsides make a good setting because they turn into gardens in late summer that beckon you on and on. I am speaking of roadsides in the spirit of going out to get wildflower pictures—not with the purpose of going somewhere. Superhighway, turnpike, throughway, and parkway are not the roadsides I am thinking of. It is almost impossible to imagine what delight awaits the person with a camera who ventures onto the dirt road. Here are a wonderful free show and setups for pictures. The late summer plant photographer should be an off-

38. A wealth of beautiful designs await macrophotography. Every detail of plant life is a masterpiece of art. Upper left: dynamic spirals in the center of a daisy; upper right: top view of milkweed floret; lower left: capsules of spirea; lower right: center of a witch hazel flower.

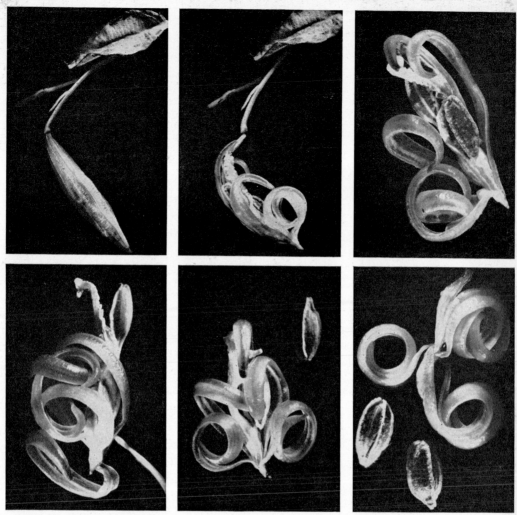

39. A series of still photographs showing an action sequence. The above series illustrates the opening of the seed pod of a touch-me-not, or jewel weed. The pod looks like a string bean. When it opens suddenly, segments coil up kicking out the seeds.

40. To get an outstanding photograph of a beautiful outdoor spot, look for an accent such as reflections in water or white birch trees.

41. On a gray, rainy day in fall or winter you can get interesting effects of tree silhouettes by shooting out of the car window.

the-concrete motorist. I hesitate to mention this because I do not want to see the little country roads crowded with traffic. But, between us friends, here is a great opportunity.

White and yellow sweet clovers are three to five feet tall. In a low place beside the road there is a gorgeous growth of purple loosestrife. Goldenrod is in its prime. The light purple clouds of flowers that bank the roadsides and edges of fields are wild bergamot, one of the most common and hauntingly beautiful. In some places, the wild bergamot has spread and flourished in the last ten years to become one of America's most charming and conspicuous flowers, competing with the asters, wild carrot (Queen Anne's lace), and chicory to own the roadsides.

Stop and explore a bit away from the road. In a damp place you will find, come September, the famous Joe-pye weed. I have never seen a note as to who Joe Pye was—perhaps a farmer who stood in front of this great flower with a shotgun to keep it from being mowed down. It towers six or eight feet, but do not look up to it when you shoot in hope of glorifying this flower against blue sky. The misty mauve of the giant flower head blends with a blue or white overcast. To make Joe-pye show in a photograph you must maneuver to have dark shadows behind it.

The bull thistle that is blooming in the dry field at the same time is more sure fire. Thistles are among our most photogenic wildflowers. They are the right height to get a 45-degree down-ward slant on them, the leaves make an artistic pattern below the flowers, and often bull thistles grow beside a good-looking boulder that adds the touch of environment. Common mullein is found at the same time and place. Its leaves have marvelous radial symmetry, and the flower stalk shoots up above, making mullein outstanding. However, mullein is more often associated with cow pies than with a nice clean boulder. It is a matter of personal taste whether you want to include the rural atmosphere in this case.

Before we leave late-summer wildflower picture hunting, I

urge every photographer to be on the alert for gentians and ladies' tresses. Gentians are considered rare. But in locations where they grow they can be very common, and uncommonly beautiful. I have found fringed and closed gentians abundant in limestone areas such as the western Berkshires, around Pittsfield and Stockbridge, Massachusetts, and in northwestern Connecticut. And the gentians are an almost universal wealth in the western mountains in late summer. Also, do you know ladies' tresses? This is one of our commonest wild orchids and grows in open fields where it is easy to find. It forms an exquisite corkscrew spiral. It is a remarkable subject for close-up photography.

Some photographer somewhere is going to go out with his camera in late fall after the asters, thistles, and goldenrods have vanished and the days are short, and catch sight of a shrub reflecting the rays of the low sun with a lovely golden gauze. That flowering shrub will be witch hazel, the most unorthodox of all our wildflowers. Because it is solitary and out of season, it is conspicuous. Witch hazel delights the eye and the spirit—but somehow it does not delight the camera. If you can take a picture of this last one in the parade of wildflowers and have it look anything like what you see, you are a much better photographer than I am. Anybody with close-up equipment can get the interesting right-angle design of this flower, but taking it on the bush, in the wild, is a real challenge. The yellow of the petals, which are very narrow, is lost in the play of light and shade that surrounds witch hazel. This brings us to some of the frustrations in photographing wildflowers and procedures which I have found to overcome them.

MAJOR PROBLEMS

It is a lovely summer day. A warm sun floods the fields and roadsides, which are alive with wildflowers—daisies, black-eyed Susans, bouncing Bets, red clovers, sky-blue chicories, honeysuckle, butter-and-eggs, and countless more—all fresh on a clear day after the showers last night. Only a slight breeze stirs the leaves. The hedgerows bear great domes of elderberry, whorls of arrowwood, and trumpets of morning glories. In low wet places meadow rue and iris are bright among the curving swords of sweet flag.

It is a perfect day to go out in your shirtsleeves, explore around the countryside, and, incidentally, shoot a few wildflower pictures. The light is excellent, there is almost no wind, the stage is set. Why not?

Yes, why not? Because, for certain reasons, the tranquillity of the wildflowers and their patiently standing still waiting for their pictures to be taken is a great illusion. If you want to relax peacefully in the fields do not plan incidentally to shoot a few wildflowers. This is particularly true if you have somebody with you standing around, while you are taking snapshots, waiting to move on. If you take flower pictures under those circumstances you will probably not have flower pictures at all but you will have a shock. When you see the negatives you will wonder why the wildflowers look so insignificant, or else you will not be able to discern any flowers at all as you remember seeing them. It is an odd perversity the way beautiful wildflowers that sprinkle the fields and roadsides at the height of the summer season all but vanish in a negative or look like unfortunate spots which should be touched out of the print.

That is because they snap out in color when you look at them but disappear among the multitude of highlights of grass and twigs and leaves in black and white. Even in color they always look smaller than you think, losing their forms and resembling nothing more than confetti.

If, after going through your disappointment and wasting some film, your pride as a photographer is hurt and you square your jaw and set out alone and unhurried to lick the problem, you can return with some good pictures. At the end of the day you will emerge in a trance, with knees and shoes muddy, clothes torn, a harsh sunburn, and a marvelous experience that is exhausting because you have been doing some intense concentration.

You will not put many different wildflowers on film in a single day because, after finding a photogenic specimen in good light, you may consume from a half hour to an hour in trying to outwit the subject.

You have to get close to a flower to take a portrait of it, even the biggest, and that tends to magnify its least movement. This is one of the greatest problems in wild-flower photography—how to get a sharp negative which can be enlarged as much as you wish. Suppose you are stalking flowers large enough so that you do not need special close-up equipment, such as extra bellows extension or a lens for getting up to within a few inches of the subject. The big flowers are the most recreation and the most fun. They make compositions against backgrounds of blue sky, clouds, trees, rocks, hedgerows, and water. Among these are the tall goldenrods, asters, day lilies, bear grass, yucca, milkweed, Joe-pye weed, thoroughwort, common mullein, chicory, and sweet clovers. They also include clumps of black-eyed Susans, daisies, lupine, morning glories, roses, blackberries, jasmine that climb on fences, and flowers like golden glow and phlox that jump out of gardens and go wild. This is good wildflower material for standard photography. But for top-notch shots you will want to get within a few feet of them or as close as your camera will focus.

The first disillusionment is when you find that flowers do not stand still waiting for their pictures to be taken. They quiver, sway, describe circles, nod, swing, and bounce up and down. However, it is my impression that there comes a time when a flower is perfectly still. That is just before you set up your tripod or point the camera in its direction. But the moment you start to focus on the flower it starts its gyrations. At that instant it becomes the plaything of every zephyr; until then the flower seemed hardly to stir on this perfect day for outdoor photography, but there is now an amazing series of local disturbances to which the subject responds with eccentric dances.

This is not entirely the cynical remark of one who has been foiled many times. There are physical reasons why, even on an otherwise still day, the flower has its own local disturbances. On a fine fair day in summer there are apt to be fleecy clouds floating about the sky. When a shadow passes over the flower the air is slightly cooler, and when the sun shines on it again it is suddenly warmer. This sets up local drafts. For the same reason the edge of woods, where many flowers are found, always has a play of air currents due to the mottled patches of sunlight and shade. If you set up your camera when the flower is under the shadow of clouds—or, vice versa, when it is in a steady light with the sun shining from blue sky—the moment you are ready to shoot the condition is reversed. The sun comes out full on your subject, or it goes under a big cloud, and at that moment the flower begins to jiggle and shake. This is one of the ways that flowers outwit photographers and it is a pattern of behavior that you must learn to cope with.

The problem of quivering would not be too serious if there were some cadence to it, as when everything shakes and then stands still. But the instant of complete equilibrium throughout the flower and all its petals and leaves is fleeting and rare. Usually there is a loosely caught petal or delicately hung leaf that persists in teasing you with its blurring vibration. You must either forget that (if it is a leaf that does not matter, pick it) and glue your eye on the principal features of the picture, or else play it for the rare instant of over-all stillness. After taking many pictures of flowers outdoors, you learn to sense the instant of quiet. But the message from eye to hand to cable release to shutter can hardly be transmitted fast enough. You see everything still, and by the time the shutter clicks it is too late.

I try to anticipate the instant of equilibrium. There is a sequence of movements—a puff of wind, a jerking play of drafts, followed by a gradual settling down of the whole thing. It is like something running swiftly downhill in your feelings. You can feel the coming of the bottom point when, for a fraction of a second, everything will be still—and then bounce up again. So *before* that instant comes, my slow-moving mind starts the message on its way and I push the cable release. Sometimes that hits it on the point, sometimes not. But with practice you catch more and more flower pictures that do not shake.

In addition to passing clouds and the play of light and shade, there is another physical reason for agitation of a flower about to have its picture taken. This is that the flower is not nervous but that you are. Most wildflowers do not grow in sublime detachment, strange as this sounds. They emerge from an interlocking jungle. This consists of stiff and awkward stalks of last year's growth that surround the base of the flower with a fantastic scaffolding. Intertwined are runners, thorny twigs that hook on to everything in reach, stiff grasses, all connected up in a mysterious way worse than a sensitive tangle of jackstraws. The slightest agitation, even several feet away from the flower, will be immediately communicated to the subject on your ground glass.

After the setting up, focusing, and making of all adjustments, the moment comes to peer closely at the flower and watch for its slightest quiver. You lean forward tensely and unconsciously change your stance. Naturally your foot touches a stick or weed stalk or grass that acts as a trigger to the scaffolding and you are amazed to see the flower move. It dodges and shies away, even leaving the field of the ground glass entirely. So you must learn not to stir your foot, and also to keep your elbows and garments close-hauled.

Of course, the question of flowers holding still and your dealing with this by anticipating the instant of stillness and keeping your feet quiet is only for wildflower portraits on gentle summer days when only the smallest breezes are stirring. If it is a windy day you had better not try to take a wildflower picture *in situ*. That is the day to go sailing or limit your plant photography to landscapes, trees, lichens, or mushrooms that grow so low and are so firmly set that neither passing clouds nor the zeal of the photographer moving his feet has any effect.

I should add that you can have another recourse in your kit, the synchronized flash. I have used flash outdoors, even in sunlight, to step up the speed to 1/250 of a second. This helps to iron out blurring. It will not overcome the healthy swaying of a breeze-tossed plant, but flash does increase the opportunities for good pictures, if you are serious and devoted to building a file of wildflower negatives or color transparencies as fast as possible. Even at best this takes time. You cannot order wildflowers to bloom for any amount of equipment and money. Those you miss one season must wait a year.

Another recourse becoming increasingly popular with plant photographers is the use of electronic flash. This insures "freezing" of all action regardless of wind. It enables you to obtain many pictures otherwise impossible. The chief problem on a very windy day is to achieve good composition, especially when trying for close-ups.

Flash in wildflower photography offers other advantages than to stop motion. It lets you work on an overcast day and in shadowy places such as in the woods, or in the shadow of a mountain or cliff. Also, by spotlighting the subject, it has pictorial value. Flowers often grow in confusing surroundings. The skillful use of flash reduces the competition of surroundings by making the background darker in contrast to the subject. Because a flashbulb attached to the camera tends to flatten out the subject, I use two flashlights on spikes with about four feet of cord. They can be placed to one side or eight feet apart on two sides, or below the camera, so as to build up depth with shadows in the flowers.

The second greatest problem for getting definition and clarity into photographs of plants concerns the skill with which all plants camouflage their leaves and flowers on the negative. This is due to the contrast of brilliance in terms of what you see. Moreover, the eye is selective through the mind, while the camera is not selective and takes in everything that light brings through the lens. Color pictures do not have this difficulty to such an extreme degree as black and white. When you translate color (as the eye sees it) into gradations of gray (as the negative sees it), the result is entirely different than that of the mental image.

For example, a common combination is yellow against green —a vivid picture as you see it. But yellow photographs dark, not light. Therefore, goldenrod, a yellow lily, golden glow, butter-and-eggs, evening primrose, and countless other flowers that you admire against green leaves or grass may be scarcely visible on the negative. You have to use extra-contrast paper to print it at all, and then you lose the soft, vivid quality of the original subject. One answer is to shoot from a low angle so as to silhouette the yellow flower against sky, not against green. Another way is to maneuver so that shadows under a tree are behind the flower. A yellow filter (I use K2) helps to build up the contrast under both methods. In fact, when taking black-and-white pictures outdoors I almost never take the filter off. It lightens yellow while it darkens the blue of the sky.

Blue flowers also offer difficulties, as they photograph so much lighter than the eye sees them. For this reason the beautiful sky-blue chicory taken against the blue sky almost vanishes in a black-and-white negative. Little blue flowers on a stone wall, or bluets that scatter so charmingly in a lawn, are scarcely distinguishable from reflections from stones and leaves of grass. The yellow filter which darkens blue makes the blue flowers unnaturally dark. Thus, for blue flowers it is better to maneuver for a green background and no filter. This gives contrast because green becomes darker and blue lighter on a black-and-white negative, and thus approximate what the eye sees.

By the same token, to bring out the details of a white and yellow flower, such as a daisy, blackberry and apple blossoms, some water lilies, asters, and garden roses, it is better to shun the filter. The yellow filter, by lightening the yellow center, will cause it to lose contrast with the white petals.

Failure to understand how colors are translated by the negative is one of the chief reasons why wild flower pictures are so often flops. The photographer may have taken excellent pictures of landscapes, dogs, babies, houses, girls, and even trees—where the subject is defined by bold contrasting lights and shadows. The peculiar effect that colors have on silver salts in the emulsion of the film plays a much more important part in photographing details of flowers or masses of color in fields and gardens where definition depends a great deal on color. This subject is discussed with authority in a book called *The Photographic Negative* by Herbert C. McKay, F.R.P.S.

Speaking of using a shadow background for contrast, one of my most useful accessories is a square of black cloth. This is to drape on the arm to throw a shadow back of the flower. Of course, any opaque object large enough to throw the shadow will do, even a hat. In composing the picture you do not necessarily want to bring the entire background into shadow; it looks more natural to have it only as part of the background, as when shadows are cast by a tree branch or bush. Usually, the best place for the shadow is behind the blossom so as to silhouette it.

Occasionally the black cloth becomes the shadow itself. You arrange it behind the flower making sure that it is far enough away to be out of focus. Otherwise it looks silly to have a sharp-edged black cloth lying on the ground or draped on other plants in the picture. You must sharpen your judgment as to whether or not the shadow is behind the flower where you want it. It is amazing how the slightest difference in stance, a few inches right or left, nearer or farther, throws you off. You must establish a straight line from the lens of the camera to the flower and see where it lines up against the background. A reflex camera makes this easier, but if the shot is close up you have to compensate for the parallax; just an inch or so between the lenses of the reflex camera makes a big difference between the relationship of the flower and its background. With a little practice you can figure out where the shadow should fall by simply stooping over and sighting along the camera as though aiming a gun. Once the place for the shadow is determined, you stand up with your black cloth, or hat, and throw the shadow on that place.

IS IT GOOD SPORTSMANSHIP TO ARRANGE THE SURROUNDINGS?

Authenticity of wildflower pictures taken outdoors in their natural habitats does not depend on leaving the surroundings untouched. Remember, you are taking a picture of a plant and not necessarily of the trash which nature has left around it, or capricious plants in the environment. You are entitled to clear away any obstruction that interferes with a good view of the subject. You are also entitled to arrange shadows, as we have just discussed, instead of accepting those which the sun is momentarily throwing. So, to do good work you may have to clear away some of the jungle of twigs, grass, and weeds that will make confusion on the negative.

If it is a small flower and you are photographing the entire plant, the ground *must* be simplified, grass pulled away, stones that reflect light removed—often just plain dark earth is the best. Also, a shadow that falls on the plant must be removed by plucking a tall weed or—judiciously—pruning a branch from a tree.

As for moving objects *into* the picture, that is not always valid. Honest natural history photography must stick to the ecology of the growing plant, that is, its native and characteristic habitat. If you add a few props, such as a stone or a pine cone, they should be picked up in the immediate neighborhood. Some years ago I saw an exhibit of superb photography in a natural history museum. But things were brought together which do not grow together. This was arranging for artistic photography, not natural history photography.

SOME MINOR PROBLEMS

In addition to the big difficulties of quivering and color in wildflower photography, there are a number of minor annoyances. The worst is a phenomenon of streaks of white or glaring white blobs that ruin a good photograph. These are caused by highlights from stones, leaves, blades of grass, or drops of water. The whole outdoors on a sunny day is a bewildering display of reflections. Yet in some freakish way you hardly notice these highlights when taking the picture, and they show up as distracting blemishes in the print.

The answer is to train yourself to see them in advance. Study every reflection in the field of the lens. If your background is a jungle of sweet flag or grass or cattails, you will have to root up a good deal of ground to get the blizzard of highlights out of the picture. So be careful whose ground you are destroying. It is better to skip that picture. The same is true of stones in a field. But more often the offending streaks and highlights are from a twig or one outlandishly long blade of grass in the background, and all you have to do is pluck it out of the picture before you shoot. An immovable stone in the distance, or glare from white or a shiny trunk of a tree, is usually coped with by merely moving your camera a foot or two right or left.

Shadows are another minor annoyance. On a partly cloudy day the shadows have a way of robbing you of more time for outdoor photography than any other frustration except talkative people. There may be plenty of blue sky with clouds looking pretty when you embark on taking a picture. But a demon is watching you. The moment you have found a breathtaking subject, and have made all your calculations, perhaps stopping to reload your camera or have a sandwich, and you are set and ready—at that instant the sky is filled with clouds and shadows rule. You wait an hour, in fact, if this is a great picture, and of course it is; you are determined to wait all day. Finally you surrender, and then, the moment you have packed everything back in the car and have abandoned the site, the sun shines beautifully.

Nevertheless, it is surprising how fast shadows thrown by a tree or other nearby object travel. You may make elaborate preparation to take a flower picture only to find it in the shadow of tree foliage, or a telegraph pole, when ready to click. If the offending shadow caster is a small tree or something narrow, just wait; your flower will be out in the sun again presently. But if you are working with a patch of sun from an opening in foliage, as often happens in the woods, work fast; your opportunity is short.

Be sure to keep the shadow of your camera, or your own head, off the plant you are taking. That is no joke. I am repeatedly having to move the tripod or duck my head. For some psychological reason you are not apt to notice a shadow like that at the time of taking the picture.

Then there is the miscellany of bothersome events that dog the heels of the outdoor plant photographer. The grass that suddenly flips in front of the lens; the twig of a bush that sticks in your eye; the tripod leg that slips at the last instant because it is in soft mushy soil; and the countless threads and hairs from spider webs, milkweed, and so on that get in front of the lens.

I recall a fine shot of cotton grass. This sedge features a silvery ball of silk with a twist and a flare most artistic when it catches light in a certain way. The one I had found had a spectacular whorl, and it was clearly a cinch. No interference from surroundings, plenty of sunlight, and a quiet nook out of the wind. Later, when the film was developed, I wondered how the negative had received such a vicious scratch that came straight out of the artistic whorl. The answer was that it was not a scratch, but a strand that had come loose and stuck straight out where it caught the glint of light. Nowadays I carry manicure scissors for such contingencies. In that case I simply did not see the stray hair until it showed up in the negative, simulating an evil scratch.

Thus far in our story we have been concerned with problems outside the plants themselves—wind which shakes them, shade which darkens them, peculiarities of the film emulsion translating color intensities different from those the eye sees, reflections from leaves and stones and drops of water, and the interference of effluvia such as spider silk, threads, and twigs that seem to be invisible until you have developed the film. But do not suppose that otherwise plants are docile and obedient models. If you are doing serious photography in this field you will soon find that plants are very active organisms.

Many flowers have unexpected ways of opening and closing. The blue-eyed grass (a very pretty purple and yellow relative of the iris that grows on a dry hillside meadow, and common where you find it) will close its eyes if it is disturbed, or the instant it does not receive a bombardment of sunlight. Chicory, the sky-blue roadside weed, also closes up when the sun goes under a cloud. The evening primrose does just the opposite; it closes as soon as the morning sun is full above the horizon and opens in the shade of evening. Recently I caught sight of a beautiful specimen of bladder campion with its lacy petals and unique bulbous pattern waiting to have its picture taken in the early morning. (Campion is a member of the pink family, to which the cultivated carnation also belongs.) I made a mental note and went back to it with my camera an hour later to find the flower in total collapse. Then, that same afternoon when the sun was behind a dark cloud, it bloomed again gloriously.

Other flowers open suddenly. Once I had before my lens a fine combination of a wide-open wild iris and beside it on the same stalk a handsome burgeoning bud. A flower and a bud together, as they are in nature, tell a better story than a single bloom alone. Therefore I fussed with this opportunity, taking plenty of time to check stop, exposure, and background—I know of no satisfaction in photography greater than to have the opportunity for unhurried study of a subject and striving for greater perfection. Before I ended all this self-indulgence, and was set for the great picture, I rubbed my eyes with disbelief. There were two irises in full bloom. The bud had popped open. Day lilies have a peculiar habit of dropping out of the picture. Day lilies, escaped from gardens, are big and beautiful along the roadside, and may be considered superb subjects for photographing. But be prepared for the day lily to drop off just before you shoot, no matter how quietly you move in its presence. The next day another one will mysteriously appear in the same place. Each day lily, well named, blooms but a few hours, and the bud next below on the stalk opens the next day.

As a last resort, moving flowers to get them into a better light or to make a better looking group may be legitimate. This is so only if the subject is not a rare and protected flower such as a wild orchid, a fringed gentian, or trailing arbutus. In that case you get flashlight equipment, take it in the shade, or pass it up. You may move flowers to make a better group if those flowers grow in groups naturally, and at that particular place they did not happen to be close enough together to be encompassed by your lens.

The hawkweeds fulfill these conditions. Indeed, the orange hawkweed, called devil's-paintbrush, is considered a pest by the farmer because it embitters the clover and grass of the pasture. But for us it is one of the most brilliantly colored of the meadow flowers, as also is the taller yellow hawkweed. Suppose you want to shift hawkweeds so as to have a number in a single frame. This calls for moving them together a matter of a few inches. But try and do it. All hawkweeds, when disturbed, will immediately let their heads fall over as though they had been hung.

The same is true of milkweed. I wonder how many people have picked those stately blooms, great handsome balls of delicately tinted lavender—or in the case of swamp milkweed, an exquisite rosy red—with fine big oval leaves like the leaves of the rubber tree or magnolia, and then been astonished to find themselves holding a limp ruin a few minutes later. You soon learn to photograph milkweed untouched where it grows, or not at all.

One of the most baffling mysteries in plant photography is the way stems vanish in photographs. The bloom or the foliage, if you are taking a spray of fall colors, seems to be suspended in mid-air, and that lends a sort of unreality to the picture. The explanation is that a stem is often shaded just below the flower or the leaves where you want to see it the most. Also, a stem is green or black so that it darkens and disappears against a dark background. The answer is simple. Light up the stem as brightly as you can with a reflection from a small mirror. One of my most useful accessories is a four-by-five-inch mirror from the top of an old fitted case. This not only brings out stems but also leaves that try to hide in the shade, and the small mirror can be used to throw searching illumination into the flower itself.

The layer of operations for wildflower photography extends from below the earth—where you may dig a hole to bring your lens vis-à-vis a violet, ground myrtle, or trailing arbutus—to the top of your car when you drive into a field to confront a gigantic sunflower or apple blossoms. In this layer for picture taking, not over fifteen feet deep, a lot of problems and frustrations await you. Plants call for all you've got to outwit them.

INDOOR PLANT PHOTOGRAPHY

Indoors also the plant photographer can enjoy an absorbing hobby, or become an expert and have a lucrative practice.

Today in every part of our country members of garden clubs and others are responding to the lure of flower arranging. The practice includes variations such as dry plant arrangements and making compositions with driftwood and contorted branches and roots. Flower arranging has achieved the status of art with exhibits and shows, where the arrangements are judged and prizes awarded according to code. People pursue this interest as seriously as the photographer pursues his—the two fit together. It would be hard to find anybody who has created an arrangement worthy of competing for a prize who would not love to have it photographed for a permanent record. Whether or not this is profitable for the photographer depends on negotiation, but at least it is an absorbing and interesting challenge for his camera and skill.

There is the question of surroundings. Often the flower arranger, interpreting a theme, will create the whole setting, and the photographer does not have to consider this point. Otherwise the photographer, unless it is a portrait of the arrangement alone suspended in a black, white, or gray vacuum, may have an interesting job of making the center of interest in a corner of the room, on a window sill, on a table, or beside a sofa or bed.

Many of the same problems we have discussed above of translating colors to black-and-white film, and an understanding of how to manipulate this with filters, which we encountered in the outdoor photography of wildflowers, are involved in taking good pictures of flower arrangements. However, with all indoor photography the manipulation of shadows is a different matter from outdoor photography, and important. You have infinite scope with shadows when using spotlights and floods. Shadows are the subtle and fluid elements which will make or spoil a photograph of a flower arrangement. The slightest change, just an inch or so, of the angle of the light will make a shadow sharper or mistier, taller or shorter. It's fun.

I enthusiastically call your attention to *macrophotography* for indoor photography of plant life, which will turn up surprising effects, and also offer an opportunity for some original scientific research.

The word comes from Greek *makro*, meaning "large." This does not refer to the subject of your photograph. Just the opposite. It refers to the relative size of the subject on the film. If this is the same size as the object being photographed (known as 1:1), obviously the subject of the picture must be very small to fit on the film. This is especially true on 35 mm, which is the most adaptable for macrophotography. If the image on the film is twice as large as the subject, namely 1:2, you have magnified it when taking it. Macro can work easily up to 1:10 in color or on fine-grain film. and that approaches low-power microscope photography. With these large images on the film you can get astonishing magnification, according to the degree of enlargement you give it when projecting either to print on paper or to throw on a screen.

From 1:½ up to 1:10 is the general working range for macrophotography, but in practice it extends in both directions to overlap on the one hand with ordinary close-up photography, and on the other hand with microphotography, as the magnification increases. However, in the direction of greater magnification of the image, macro does not technically become micro as long as you use incidental lighting. Incidental lighting means illuminating the object so that it is seen by light bouncing back into the camera—this is the way our eyes see things, and it makes them appear natural. But true micro uses transmitted lighting, shining through translucent material. This makes it look diagrammatic and "unnatural," as when viewed through a microscope.

Taking this range up to ten diameters of magnification as the ideal for macrophotography, consider what the Plant Kingdom has to offer the explorer. It is an arresting fact that nature creates trees, flowers, ferns, mushrooms, and all plants as beautiful objects with over-all qualities of streamlining, proportion, balance, and dynamic symmetry.

Stand off and look at a tree. It is fluid and beautiful as a whole. Nonessentials are eliminated. It is an honest expression of a purely utilitarian mechanism, well planned, with its parts grouped and all in the right proportion and weight. The tree operates silently, efficiently, and continuously.

But there is a marvelous fact about that tree—or flower—which you may not realize when viewing it as a whole. Every detail down to a single cell is an equally perfect unit, operating more or less independently, although coordinated with the total plant. Every part, large and small, has those qualities of art which are found in utility, fitness, economy, and the perfect adaptation of the means to the end. Exploring inward, you see the leaf, vein pattern, bud, leaf scar, markings in bark, fashion of twig, cone, fruit, seed, sepal, petal, stamen, nectar guide, pod, capsule, pollen jewelry, seed wings or parachutes, hairs, tubes, details of grouping and architecture, and a thousand other marvelous little things, each of which can make a photograph. Perhaps it will be a botanical study or perhaps sheer objective art of color and form, or abstract art. I have made murals five feet long of plant parts one-quarter inch in size, and I defy anybody to identify what they are. The rhythm and curves are amazing.

That is your treasury for machrophotography. The trouble is that life is not long enough to finish the job of taking such pictures, once you start.

It is impossible in this space to delineate all the ways and means for the macrophotography of plants. A basic approach is as follows:

1. *A 35 mm Camera.* Larger cameras can be used, but they require larger bellows and they are more awkward to handle and support firmly when dealing with tiny subjects.

2. *A Firm Support.* A nonwobbly table and a vertical column

on which an arm to hold the camera slides up and down for focusing. You can take macro pictures horizontally, or at any angle. But it is important to have the plane of the object parallel to the plane of the film. The quickest and surest way to do this is to shoot straight down. Also, the subject has less vibration when it is resting on something.

3. *Extension Tubes* (or bellows). These extend the distance between the lens and the film. The larger the image you desire, the longer the extension—and conversely, the shorter the distance between the lens and the subject. This means that a very small object (for example, the tip of a stamen) calls for a longer extension that comes into focus when the lens is only an inch or two from the subject. The larger the subject (for example, a flower the size of a daisy), the shorter the extension, and the lens may be six inches from the subject when it comes into focus.

4. *The Lens*. Any standard lens mounted with a shutter to stop down for depth of focus. I work mostly with a Tessar F 3.5 between f 16 and f 22. Also, I have a low-power microscope objective corrected for use without an eyepiece (the camera is the eye) which stops down through a pinhole to f 64. But there are plenty of pictures to take with less magnification and normal stops, so I seldom use this.

5. *Ground-glass focusing*. Substitute a ground-glass focusing device in place of camera. Then take it off and put the camera in its place. For precise work I use a magnifying glass above the ground glass.

6. *Light Source*. I use 6.5-volt microscope lights with condensers to narrow the beam to a spot the size of a dime. With a battery of four, mounted on movable ball-joint stands, I can throw the light from any angle and distance. Lighting is the secret of excellent macro work. Often I photograph with one light from a low angle to sharpen the shadows for definition. Larger subjects or exceptional situations call for all four lights. The adjustment of the lighting and study on the ground glass are the time-

consuming elements. For color use artificial-light-type film. For black and white use filters, depending on the color of the subject. (See discussion of this under wildflower photography earlier in this chapter.) Filters affixed to the lights do a better job than when affixed to the lens.

Narrow-beam lights are hot. You may have to focus with an ordinary desk lamp, or work fast if the subject is delicate and curls when it dries. This problem of heat is one of the peskiest, and you must solve it with your own ingenuity.

For larger subjects, or over-all illumination of a surface, such as a leaf, an ordinary floodlamp can be used. I put a No. 1 flood in a gooseneck desk lamp with its regular metal reflector, and hold this in one hand, looking at the subject and lighting it to taste, with the cable release in the other hand.

7. *Supporting the Object.* One way is to lay the object on a glass stand built by means of a double-sized microscope slide glass mounted as a transparent table with regular-sized slides for legs. Use clear cement. Make sure the glass is clean and free of dust before taking the picture. As blowing off the dust may move the object, a No. 0 camel's-hair brush is useful for removing dust specks. The little glass "table" rests on black suède paper—or any color, even white if you want a white background. The paper is out of focus but can be made to produce black, white, gray, or color backgrounds according to the way you light it with one of your narrow-beam lamps.

If the object is on a firm stem (for example, a bud or twig) it can be held out horizontally from any holder on hand. For many subjects I use a test-tube holder that has a clamp.

A small object, such as a pistil, stamen, or seed, may be held with a needle, the other end of which is stuck in a cork. This eliminates the problem of specks of dust on the glass. But be sure the needle does not show. Macrophotographs of things stuck on pins, which look like steel pipes, are not good practice.

TIME LAPSE IN STILL PICTURES

The phrase "time lapse" is borrowed from movie photography, but the still-picture photographer of plant life can use the same idea with telling effect. The time interval is longer, and the result is a series of photographs that can be exhibited side by side, or projected one after the other.

An interesting idea is to stake out a spot that has year-round identification, such as a road, stream, mountains, or tree trunks. Then take a picture from exactly the same spot at intervals, for example, once a month, or just four times a year at the height of each season.

I have photographs of a little pond with three birches taken that way and it is exciting to compare the various seasons. Also I have a sequence of a road showing how the shadows and colors of the seasons change. One of the most surprising is a series where a brook tumbles out of the woods. In winter it is an utterly different looking place from what it is in midsummer. This system can be used with macro to show buds opening. This interprets life instead of an instantaneous moment. Plants are always changing: leaves expand and fall, flowers open and then fall off when the fruit appears. You do not have to leave all this excitement to the movie man.

EXTRA REWARDS FOR THE
PLANT PHOTOGRAPHER

The presence of friendly life in beautiful color and design is reassuring in a tense and worried world. While he is really concentrating and fascinated, the plant photographer resolves all his worries. At the same time it is great sport, with challenging frustrations in dealing with shadows, with poison ivy, with flowers just out of reach in a swamp, with vibration, and with cows and cranky people. Once I was chased by a Pennsylvania farmer, flourishing a gun, when trying to take a picture of his apple blossoms. (Get permission when trespassing. But do not offer a print as a token of your good will because the owner may think you are there to sell the picture, and will resist you.)

There are many exciting by-products of discovery. A spider catches a grasshopper before your eyes. You find a black-eyed Susan with deep red rays. A myxomycete mushroom walks across a stump. A bee dives into a fringed gentian. There is an oak, chartreuse with early spring flowers, spotlighted in bright sun against a dark purple thunderstorm. A tall elm and an apple tree in full bloom side by side. They were never to be seen again. The elm was stricken with the Dutch elm disease, and the apple died.

Always take the picture when you see it. You will never have the chance again.

Finally, know what you are looking at. Get a flower book and a tree book, and take them with you.

ARE THERE ANY QUESTIONS?

Q. What cameras do you use?

A. For all macro and outdoor color I depend on Contax. I have three, all with Tessar f 3.5 lens. One is loaded for outdoor color, one for indoor color with macro, and one for black-and-white macro. I also have a Rolleiflex for general flashlight and outdoor work, and a 4 x 5 Graphic view "monorail" for outstanding color outdoors and for studio work.

Q. What equipment do you use for outdoor close-up?

A. The Rolleiflex on a short tripod, about one foot above the ground, equipped with Proxar lenses, does an excellent job in black and white, with or without flash. Also the same stand used for macro indoors can be set up outdoors with pins to hold it steady to the ground. A great deal of my close-up color work outdoors has been done with the Contax on this macro setup, using sunlight.

Q. What is your macro setup?

A. Many manufacturers make them today. I use the Zeiss

large copying stand, but substitute my own lighting system with Spencer (American Optical Company) condenser 6.5-volt mike lamps. The Zeiss focusing head is the part that holds the camera, and there are three lengths of tubes that can be used separately or fastened together for extra-long extension. I have introduced a micrometer focusing device into the system for precise work, but this is not essential.

Q. What do you say is the chief factor for successful photography?

A. First, know your subjects. Second, take lots of pictures and write down the *f* opening and the exposure for each. Then compare the result with the data. For macro you cannot successfully use a light meter. It takes a certain number of trials to sense the correct exposure. Taking macro pictures is a knack learned by practice, like playing the typewriter or tennis. After a while you can guess close to the right exposure by judging the brightness of the image on the ground glass.

TECHNICAL DATA ON
PHOTOGRAPHS

FRONTISPIECE

Wilson's Plover: 4 x 5 Graflex; 17 inch Dallon telephoto; 1/30, f 11.

BIRDS

1. *Laughing Gulls:* 4 x 5 Graflex; 8 inch Zeiss Tessar lens; 1/200, f 16, yellow filter.
2. *Western Gull:* 4 x 5 Graflex; 12 inch Dallon lens; 1/110, f 16, yellow filter.
3. *Wood Ibis:* 4 x 5 Graflex; 17 inch Dallon telephoto; 1/200, f 11, yellow filter.
4. *Screech Owl:* 4 x 5 Speed Graphic; 127 mm Kodak Ektar lens; 1/200, f 16; 2 #22 flash bulbs.
5. *Snowy Egret:* 4 x 5 Graflex; 17 inch Dallon telephoto; 1/125, f 16, yellow filter.
6. *White-throated Sparrow:* 4 x 5 Speed Graphic; 127 mm Kodak Ektar lens; 1/100, f 22; 2 #22 flash bulbs.
7. *American Egret:* 4 x 5 Graflex; 17 inch Dallon telephoto; 1/110, f 16, yellow filter.

MAMMALS

8. *Red Squirrel:* 4 x 5 Speed Graphic; 127 mm Kodak Ektar lens; 1/200, f 22; 2 #22 flash bulbs.
9. *Raccoon:* 4 x 5 Graflex; 17 inch Dallon telephoto; 1/40, f 16, yellow filter.
10. *Finback Whales:* 4 x 5 Graflex; 12 inch Dallon lens; 1/110, f 16.
11. *White-tailed Deer:* 4 x 5 Graflex; 17 inch Dallon telephoto; 1/40, f 11, yellow filter.

MAMMALS

12. *Eastern Chipmunk:* 4 x 5 Speed Graphic; 8¼ inch Goerz Dagor lens; 1/100, f 22; 2 #22 flash bulbs, gray beaver board placed 2 ft. behind stone wall.

13. *Bison:* 4 x 5 Graflex; 12 inch Dallon lens; 1/40, f 16, yellow filter.

14. *Armadillo:* 4 x 5 Graflex; 17 inch Dallon telephoto; 1/40, f 16, yellow filter.

AMPHIBIANS AND REPTILES

15. *Male Toad:* Leica; focaslide with 135 mm lens; f 12.5; open flash #11 flashbulb.

16. *Salamander eggs:* Leica; 50 mm lens; f 12.5.

17. *Embryo Red-backed Salamanders:* Leica; focaslide and extension tubes with 135 mm lens, 1/10, f 11.

18. *Quizzical pair of salamanders:* Leica; focaslide and extension tubes with 135 mm lens, f 16, open flash #5 flashbulb.

19. *Rare albino salamander:* Leica; focaslide and extension tubes with 135 mm lens; f 16; open flash #5 flashbulb.

20. *Portrait of a Copperhead:* Leica; bellows with 135 mm lens; f 22; electronic flash.

21. *Texas Horned Toad:* Leica; bellows with 135 mm lens, f 22, electronic flash (photographed in New York Zoological Garden).

22. *Roofed Turtle:* Leica; bellows with 135 mm lens, f 18, electronic flash (photographed in New York Zoological Garden).

INSECTS

23–29. All pictures were taken with a 1952 Exakta VX equipped with metal extension tubes and a 50 mm F 2.8 Tessar lens (without filters). All were illuminated with a standard Strobonar V electronic flash. Film was Plus X developed in Microdol, 68°/16 min., with constant agitation. Camera was constantly set at 1/50th with a lens aperture of f 22. The flash lamp position was varied with each subject. All pictures were "freehand" (without tripod).

MARINE LIFE

30. *Diver-photographer:* Rolleiflex; Ektachrome film, 1/125, f 5.6.
31. *Sea Urchin and Sting Ray:* Rolleiflex; Ektachrome film, 1/125, f 4.
32. *Snapper in Gorgonian garden:* Rolleiflex; Super XX film, 1/60, f 8.
33. *Spiny Lobster:* Rolleiflex; Super XX film, 1/60, f 8.
34. *Brain Coral:* Rolleiflex, Super XX film, 1/60, f 8.
35. *French Angelfish:* Rolleiflex; Super XX film; 1/60, f 8.
36. *Bluestriped Grunts:* Rolleiflex; Super XX film, 1/60, f 8.
37. *Sea Garden:* Rolleiflex; Super XX film, 1/60, f 8.

PLANTS

38. *Beautiful designs in macrophotography:* Zeiss Ikon Contax II; Tessar 1:3.5, F 5 cm lens; Agfa Finopan film; 2 secs., f 16; lighting with 2 Spencer microscope lamps, 6.5 watts each, with condenser throwing 1 in. beam. Camera mounted on Zeiss large copying stand with focusing head and 1:1 tube extension.
39. *Action sequence, opening of a Touch-me-not:* Zeiss Ikon Contax II; Tessar, 1:3.5, F 5 cm lens; Agfa Finopan film; 1 sec., f 8; lighting with 2 Spencer microscope lamps, 6.5 watts each, with condenser throwing 1½ in. beam. Camera mounted on Zeiss large copying stand with focusing head and 1:1 tube extension.
40. *Reflections in water:* Rolleiflex; Tessar 1:3.5, F 7.5 cm lens; Ansco supreme film; 1/100, f 11; K2 filter.
41. *Tree silhouettes:* Rolleiflex; Tessar 1:3.5, F 7.5 cm lens; Ansco Supreme film; 1/100, f 11; K2 filter.

INDEX

Set in Linotype Baskerville
Format by John Rynerson
Manufactured by The Haddon Craftsmen, Inc.
Published by HARPER & BROTHERS, *New York*